The Joy of Programming PHP

Table of Contents

1

Introduction

Introduction

This book is for the developer who has just come across PHP and is wondering what the big deal is, and also for the non-programmer who is just starting out— and doesn't know where to begin.

As Confusius once wisely said, *"I hear and I forget. I see and I remember. I do and I understand."* This book will get you **doing**. The book is presented as a case study of "Sam's Used Cars," and you'll be building a web site for Sam's business as we go along. Take the time and do the exercises. Struggle a little before you look up the answers.

Speaking of the answers, the companion web site to this book is http://www.joyofphp.com where you can find all the code snippets (and answers to the exercises) from this book—plus some extra goodies. If you like the book, please locate it on Amazon.com and give it a favorable review. If you don't like it, or find something that you think needs to be fixed, or you have an idea for *"More Joy of PHP"*, please email me at AlanForbes@Outlook.com

What is PHP? introduces PHP in its many and varied contexts. It explains the difference between a PHP server, a PHP file, and PHP the language. It also describes the point of PHP, which is to create dynamic web pages.

Installing and Configuring PHP describes how to install and configure PHP on your own computer. Of course, you can't do much PHP programming if you don't have PHP so this is an important prerequisite to the rest of the book.

Introduction to HTML lays the groundwork by discussing HTML. PHP is a language that modifies and generates HTML, so you have to know HTML as the foundation for using PHP to modify HTML. We cover required and optional tags, plus enough extras to get you going.

Basic PHP Syntax Introduces the language of PHP. Here we show how to intersperse PHP and HTML in the same file, and what to expect when you do so.

Some Fun Right Away gives you a chance to try out some PHP before we go much further, to give you an early sense of the joy you are going to experience when you master it.

Editors and Staying Organized talks about how to actually edit a PHP file, and guides readers towards some of the tools available to make editing easy to do so. Also, staying organized is a good habit to start off with.

Next we discuss *Variables, Numbers, Dates, and Strings*. This chapter covers how to create and use a variable in PHP, as well as how to perform arithmetic and useful numeric functions. It covers strings and useful string functions, and also covers dates and date functions. It also describes how to read the PHP documentation when you need more.

The chapter on *Control Structures* covers how to add conditional logic to your application, and how to perform repeatable tasks in an automated fashion.

The chapter *How to use a database, specifically mySQL* is content heavy. Here you learn what a database is, how tables work, and how to work with SQL statements. I also introduce the tool PHPMyAdmin, which is a great tool to help you get started with mySQL. We introduce Sam, the used car salesman, who wants a web site that allows visitors to see what cars he has for sale, without having to constantly tweak the HTML of his site. Sam's Used Cars will be a database-driven web site.

In the chapter *Using mySQL and PHP Together* we begin to tie the two topics together and use PHP and mySQL simultaneously to create truly dynamic web sites.

As we progress through our case study, we'll shift from theory to practice. The chapter *Creating forms to Display, Add, Edit, and Delete data* starts to put some of our theory into practice by creating specific examples of web pages that perform actions on our database.

Session Variables allow you to create a variable to store a value that you can use anywhere in your web site. For instance, when you log into Amazon.com, you'll notice that every page says '*Welcome, Alan*' or something similar— except, of course, with your name rather than mine. Session variables offer one way to achieve this effect in PHP.

A used car web site wouldn't be of much value if you couldn't see pictures of the cars, so in the chapter *Working with Images* we cover powerful techniques for using your database to associate specific cars with specific images.

PHP File Uploads. Building on the previous chapter on images, we extend our web site's functionality to allow users to upload images of the cars directly from a browser, rather than having to copy the images to the hard drive.

All languages have their quirks, and *PHP Quirks and Tips* introduces some of the features of PHP that might seem odd to some.

Finally, we discuss *Security Considerations.* Security shouldn't be an afterthought when building a web application, but it did come last in the book only because you can't secure something unless you first understand how it works. Don't skip this chapter!

Praise for "The Joy of PHP"

"I'm probably categorized as an 'inexperienced' programmer. I'm pretty good with VBA in MS Access. I've been wanting to learn to use a 'real' programming language & I think PHP is the way to go (which is why I backed your book!).

That said, I've been incredibly impressed with your book. Everything you have does a great job of slowly adding new things!"

- Matt R.

2

What is PHP?

PHP is a programming language you can use to create web applications. It's free, powerful, relatively easy to set up and learn, and it has extensions and frameworks available to do almost anything you could imagine. You can get started quickly, and you won't outgrow it later when you get really good at it. In my humble opinion, PHP is a great language that will be well worth it the time and effort you put into learning it.

Frankly, it's just *plain fun* too. That's what inspired me to write this book.

Let's get started. The most basic concept you need to grasp is that a web page is just a bunch of text, organized in a certain way, which is displayed by a browser. Only a few companies make browsers, but millions of people make web pages—and so can you.

Most computer programs need some way to know if a file is intended for them or not. In the PC world, this is accomplished by file extensions. (Bear with me, this next bit *is* relevant). For example, a file named "my book.**docx**" is associated with Microsoft Word because its extension (the text following the dot) is "docx". Similarly, a PowerPoint file might end with .ppt or .pptx. Other programs also have their own unique extensions.

A web page typically, but not exclusively, has an extension such as .htm or

.html to indicate that it is an HTML file. An HTML file can be on your own computer, or on a different computer somewhere out on the Internet. The browser doesn't care. Here's a simple example of an html file out on the Internet:

http://www.tsowell.com/columns.htm

This was about the simplest web page I could find...just two links to other pages. Go ahead and visit it. Notice that the last three characters are .htm, which indicates that it is an HTML file intended for display in a browser. If that file were on your local computer, for instance in your "My Documents" folder, all you would have to do to see it in a browser would be to double-click on it.

Your browser would know how to do the rest and you would see something like this:

- Current and Archived Columns

- Books of Collected Columns

This *particular* file is not on your local computer, however. It is on a **server** out on the Internet. So how does the file get into your browser when you click on it? At the risk of oversimplifying it, you don't have to worry about that part so much. The other computer, known as the "web server", has the file and it knows how to get it to you.

In the case of an HTML file such as this one, the server sends the file **as is** without doing *anything* to it. In other words, the file that the browser **gets** is *exactly the same* as the file on the file system, regardless of whether it was originally on your computer or on the server.

We would call this a *static* web page.

Introducing PHP

Now let's add PHP to the picture. PHP has several meanings depending on the context in which it is used, so I'm going to try to explain them all. There is a "**PHP server**", which is a web server which is running PHP software on it. Let's contrast a PHP server with a "plain" server, one that is not running PHP. A "plain" web server just takes a request from a browser, locates the appropriate file, and sends it to the browser *as is*, with no manipulation. In other words, it only serves **static** web pages.

Once you add PHP to a web server, you get additional functionality—without taking any existing functionality away. The server can still continue to send static HTML files to the browser, but it can also **manipulate** the files *prior to* sending them to the browser.

A file that has been manipulated prior to being sent to the browser is referred to as a **dynamic** web page.

> A **static web page** never changes, unless a *person* specifically edits the page.
>
> A **dynamic web page** can be different every time it is viewed by a browser, because the *server* edits the page prior to sending it to the browser, according to what instructions the programmer has coded into that specific page.

Example

Here's an example. Let's say you have a web page on which you wanted the current date to appear. With a static web page, you would have to go in and edit the page every single day to update the date. That would get tiresome pretty quick!

The HTML code would look something like this:

```
<html>
<body>
Hello world! Today's date is the 7th of October 2012
</body>
</html>
```

With PHP you can let the server make the changes for you. In other words, PHP can dynamically add the correct date to the page every time the page is served if you insert a little bit of PHP code like this:

```
<html>
<body>
Hello world! Today's date is the <?php echo date('jS \o\f F Y'); ?>
</body>
</html>
```

Notice that the static text 7th of October 2012 has been replaced with <?php echo date('jS \o\f F Y'); ?>. What we did was substitute the static text with **code** that will be converted into static text by the server. (Sneak preview— PHP code appears in line with normal HTML code and is identified by appearing within **<?php** and **?>** tags).

If you happened to open those two files using your browser on the 7th of October 2012, the HTML of the two pages would be exactly the same.

But on the 8th of October, the server takes the code above and turn it into this HTML:

```
<html>
<body>
Hello world! Today's date is the 8th of October 2012
</body>
</html>
```

And the cool thing is that it works **every day**, without any further manipulation. Are you starting to see the joy?

How does a server know whether a page should be dynamic or static? An ordinary server only knows static pages. A PHP server knows that a file **should** be manipulated (it is dynamic) if it is "**PHP file**" and that it **should not** be manipulated (it is static) if it is an HTML file.

What's the difference between an HTML file and a PHP file? A PHP file is basically just an HTML file with some code inside it that tells the server to swap out the code part and insert text (or HTML) in its place. A PHP file is "just" an HTML file that has been saved with a different extension — ".php". Here's an example:

http://php.net/manual/en/tutorial.firstpage.php

> A **PHP file** is just an HTML file saved using a **.php** extension instead of an **.html** or **.htm** extension, which tells the server to look in the page for code.

What is the "extra code" that goes inside a PHP file instructing the page to be manipulated? That's **PHP the language**, which tells the server *how* and *where* the page should be manipulated prior to sending it to the browser. In other words, PHP is a programming language that is used to create dynamic web pages.

> PHP is a language that can be used to create dynamic web pages. In fact, that is the **whole point** of PHP.

How does the server know which parts of the page should be static and which parts should be dynamic? In general, the server leaves the page alone. However, if it sees the text **<?php** then all the text that follows will be treated like code, until it comes to a **?>** which signals the server to go back to sending the page as is.

> Text on a PHP page is normally static. The PHP server will dynamically convert the text that appears in between <?php and ?> tags into static text, *after* evaluating what the code means.

A little history

PHP was originally created by Rasmus Lerdorf in 1995. The main implementation of PHP is now produced by The PHP Group and serves as the formal reference to the PHP language. PHP is free software released under the PHP License, which is incompatible with the GNU General Public License (GPL) due to restrictions on the usage of the term PHP.

While PHP originally stood for Personal Home Page, it is now said to stand for PHP: Hypertext Preprocessor, a recursive acronym.

3

Installing and Configuring PHP

Introduction

Before you can begin using PHP, you need to have a copy of it. For the purposes of this book, we're going to install PHP on your local computer so you can play around with it without too much fuss.

Note that applications you write on your local computer can only be used on your local computer, or by other computers on your local network.

For the rest of this book, we are going to need Apache, MySQL, and PHP. Together, this collection is referred to as AMP. When you run this on Linux, it's called LAMP, and when you run it on Windows, it's called WAMP. Some people call this combination a "stack", and may refer to the combination as the "LAMP Stack".

Fortunately, this is a very popular combination and you don't have to figure it all out on your own.

Windows Users

As a Windows user myself, I can personally vouch for the ease of installation

and use of WampServer, which can be found at
http://www.wampserver.com/en/

> "WampServer is a Windows web development environment. It allows you
> to create web applications with Apache2, PHP and a MySQL database.
> WampServer also includes a program called **PhpMyAdmin** which allows
> you to easily manage your databases."

As part of the installation, the "www" directory will be automatically created
(usually at c:\wamp\www)

Create a subdirectory in "www" and put your PHP files inside that folder.

Using WampServer

Once WampServer is installed, you start it by selecting start WampServer
from the Windows Start menu, as shown below:

If it is not on your Start menu, search for programs that start with WAM, as
shown below:

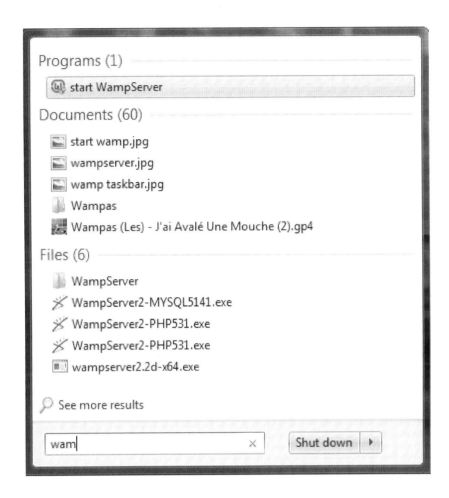

Running WAMP doesn't do anything particularly obvious. All it does is add a desktop icon on the right side of the Task bar, circled here in red:

The icon will be red if WampServer is not running, and green if it is running. Clicking on the icon will bring up a pop-up menu, similar to the Windows start menu.

Click on the "localhost" link in the WampSever menu or open your Internet browser and go to the URL http://localhost

Mac Users

According to the people who make it, XAMPP for Mac OS X is the simplest, most practical and most complete web server solution for Mac OS X. (I'm sure they have their biases, but I admire their spirit!) The distribution includes an Apache 2 web server, integrated with the latest builds of MySQL, PHP and Perl. It comes as a Mac OS X Installer package that contains all the necessary files and requires no dependencies.

If you are an experienced web developer or a Mac enthusiast who needs to run a web server, create dynamic webpages or use databases, this is your lucky day!

This version is for Mac OS X 10.4 (Intel&PPC) and higher.

XAMPP can be found at http://www.apachefriends.org/en/xampp-macosx.html

How Do I Know it is Working?

OK that was easy, but how can you check that everything really works? Just type in the following URL at your favorite web browser:

http://localhost

Windows users will see something like this:

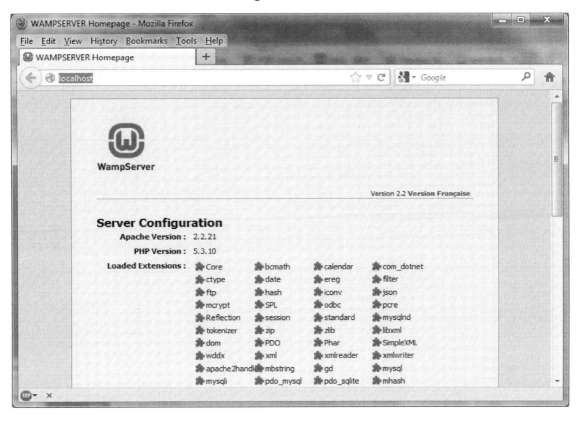

Mac users will see something like this:

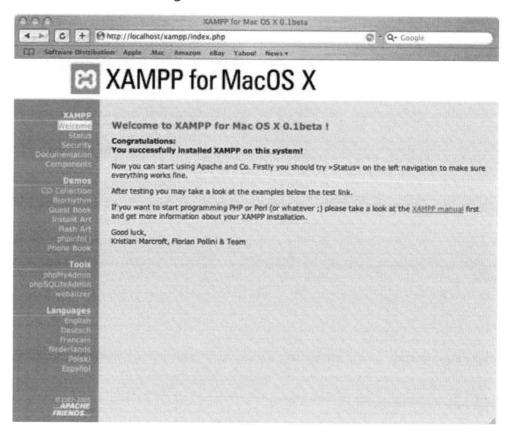

Oracle VM Virtual Box

If you are proficient with computers, you might like to try out a pre-configured virtual machine. Oracle VirtualBox is free for you to use, and folders can be shared between the host and guest machine allowing you to simply save the file you are working on and refresh your browser, there's no need to upload via FTP/SFTP to test your changes. If this sounds like a good option for you, I found a good tutorial on the subject at http://munkyonline.co.uk/blog/lamp-ubuntu-server-virtualbox.

Using Oracle Virtual Box is outside the scope of this book.

Installing for a Web Site

If you want to make your application available to everybody via the Internet, you'll need to install PHP and your application onto a publicly accessible server.   Typically that means finding a hosting provider.

If you are looking for an inexpensive hosting provider, my own PHP-based site (which makes it easy for people to write their own Kindle books at http://www.KindleSmith.com) is hosted at AccuWeb Hosting, and I haven't had any problems with them.

If you'd like to use them too, I would appreciate if you use my affiliate link at https://manage.accuwebhosting.com/aff.php?aff=743

Using the above link won't cost you any more, and I'll get a small commission on the sale. Thank you.

This topic is covered a bit more in Appendix A: Installing PHP on a Website.

Exercise

Use your editor (for instance, Programmers' Notepad) to create a file containing the following line:

```
<?php echo phpversion(); ?>
```

Save the file as phpinfo.php in the correct place on your hard drive (for instance, C:\wamp\www).

Finally, open the file with a browser by typing http://localhost/phpinfo.php

Introduction to HTML

Introduction

As we have described it, PHP is a language used for creating dynamic web pages. Web pages are written in HTML, and PHP is used so that the HTML in a given page changes depending on certain situations that you define.

Since PHP is used to **generate** the HTML on a page, it only makes sense that you need to understand basic HTML before you can go any further.

Cascading Style Sheets (CSS) is a related technology used to define the look and feel of an HTML page. Sometimes CSS is referred more simply as a style sheet.

If you already understand HTML and CSS, you can skip ahead to the next chapter.

Basic HTML

HTML is the primary building block of the web and so it is crucial to have a basic understanding of what HTML is and how it works. HTML is a markup language that is used by browsers so that they know how to render a document as a web page. Regardless of whether a document starts off as HTML written by hand or is generated using ASP, JSP, or PHP, *ultimately* the document is turned into HTML and sent to the browser to be rendered for display to a person.

HTML is a markup language that defines the structure and outline of a document and offers a structured content. Markup is not intended to define the look and feel of the content on the page beyond rudimentary concepts such as headers, paragraphs, and lists.

The presentation attributes of HTML have all been deprecated, which is a fancy word for 'please don't use these anymore, even though they still work'. The current best practices in HTML page design stipulate that most style should be contained in style sheets, which are a set of rules that describe how a page should look. Style sheets are a topic in themselves, and not very important at this stage in your learning. However, you'll want to put style sheets on your future reading list.

Writing and viewing HTML is incredibly easy (and fun), which of course is a big factor in what made it so popular. If you are reading this document on a computer, then you already have **everything** you need to try it out right now. All you need to build a web page (an HTML page) is a computer, a text editor (something as simple as Notepad will suffice) and a browser. To work with HTML you don't need a server or any special software at all. You simply create the file, save it with an .htm or .html extension, and open it directly in your browser.

> Windows users will find Programmer's Notepad to be a great editor for creating HTML files.

Basic Elements of HTML

All HTML based documents have the same basic elements. They are composed of tags that define the various parts of the document—from where it starts and ends to everything in between. HTML uses elements ("tags") to mark up sections of text. These can include headings, subtitles, lists, bold or underlined text and, of course, links. HTML documents read from left to right and top to bottom.

Tags

To distinguish tags from ordinary text, tags appear inside brackets: < and >. Most tags have an open and close tag, also known as a start and end tag. The open tag starts with < and end tag starts with </. For example **** indicates to start bold and **** indicates to stop (end) bold.

For example here is a paragraph element:

```
<p>This is the first paragraph.</p>
```

In this example the **<p>** and **</p>** are the tags; they are used to delineate the text contained within as a paragraph. Something worth pointing out here is that you don't have to put everything on a single line. The code above works just as well as this below:

```
<p>
 This is the first paragraph
</p>
```

In fact, the indentation isn't needed either, although it certainly improves the readability. Keep in mind that someone (maybe you) may have to edit your HTML in the future so making it readable is a good idea.

All tag formats are the same. They begin with a less-than sign: < and end with a greater-than sign: >. Always. What goes inside the < and > is the tag name. A big part of learning HTML is learning the specific tags and what they do.

Nested Tags

In general, most tags can be nested inside other tags, but of course there may be exceptions to this rule.

Here you see the bold tag nested inside of a paragraph tag:

```
<p>
 This is the first paragraph, with some <b>bold</b> text in it.
</p>
```

Not all elements have both an opening and closing piece. For example, <br> doesn't have a corresponding </br>, and neither does <hr>.

The <hr> tag inserts a horizontal rule (line) and the <br> tag inserts a new line.

Required tags

An HTML page starts with the <html> tag and ends with </html>. The body of the page goes inside body tags.

```
<!DOCTYPE html>
<html>
<body>
<p>This is my first paragraph.</p>
</body>

</html>
```

DocType

If a webpage is missing a <DOCTYPE> tag or has some sort of "transitional" doctype tag, the page will be rendered in what is called 'quirks' mode. Quirks mode is somewhat unpredictable, and you don't always get what you expect.

So, it is important to have a doctype tag if you want your web page to display in Standards mode, as expected. For simplicity, however, the examples in the book will skip this.

Head

The head of the document is where the **Title** and **Meta** information will go. Generally, you would also put any CSS styles, script tags, and link tags to external files in the Head also, if you have any.

```
<!DOCTYPE html>
<html>
<head>
  <title>
    This is the title of the page.
  </title>
</head>
<body>
  The body text goes here.
</body>
</html>
```

Optional Tags

Meta Tags

The Meta tag, along with the link tag, are unique in that they are the only HTML tags that require neither a closing tag nor a closing / at the end of the tag and are still considered syntactically correct.

The other thing about meta tags is that they are the only tag that, generally speaking, has no effect on the layout or processing of the page; they are used to give information about the page and/or site being viewed. The meta tag is essentially a key/value pair, and each tag can only contain one pair of values. Meta tags are used primarily by search engines.

Useful Tags

Headers

Headers are used to organize information into hierarchical groupings.

<h1>Heading1</h1>

<h2>Heading2</h2>

<h3>Heading3</h3>

<h4>Heading4</h4>

<h5>Heading5</h5>

<h6>Heading6</h6>

Header tags are block-level elements, meaning they take up an entire line by themselves, and no other markup is allowed inside heading tags.

DIV

The DIV tag is one you can use to create a logical division within your document. DIVs work with CSS, and allow you to write CSS rules that specify how the text within the DIV should be formatted.

Images/Picture

To add an image to your document, you use the "image" tag. To insert an image into your html document use the following syntax:

```
<img src="smiley.gif" alt="Smiley face">
```

The value that you put in the 'src=' attribute can either specify a graphic that is on the local file system, or you can specify a full URL which retrieves the image from somewhere else on the Internet.

Links

A link takes a user to another place when they click on it. The link can be to a specific part of the open document or to a new page entirely.

Takes the user to a new page.

```
<a href="http://www.joyofphp.com">Visit Joy of PHP!</a>
```

Takes the user to a different place (as indicated by the tag <a id="top">) in the current page:

```
<a href="#top">Go to top</a>
```

Lists

There are two kinds of lists— ordered and unordered. An **ordered** list is numbered, such as 1, 2, 3, while an **unordered** list is a list of bullet items. There are tags to start and stop the list, and tags for each item in the list.

An ordered list starts with the <ol> tag. An unordered list starts with the <ul> tag. Each list item, regardless of list type, starts with the <li> tag and ends with </li>.

```
<ul>
<li>Coffee</li>
<li>Milk</li>
</ul>
```

An ordered list: An unordered list:

1. The first list item	• Coffee
2. The second list item	• Tea
3. The third list item	• Chocolate Milk

Exercise

Make a couple of basic HTML files and place them in the correct location on your computer so that you can open them in a browser. Include lists, paragraphs, and both bold and italic text. I haven't told you how to make task italic. Given that the tag for bold is <b>, what do you suppose is the tag for italic?

HTML Tables

Tables are awesome. They solve a lot of problems, but should not be used for *overall* page layout. HTML tables should only be used for rendering data that belongs in a grid or in other words where the data describe a number of objects that have the same properties. For example, if it makes sense to display the data in Microsoft Excel, use a table.

Tables are defined with the <table> tag. A table is divided into rows (with the <tr> tag), and each row is divided into data cells (with the <td> tag). td stands for "table data," and holds the content of a data cell. A <td> tag can contain text, links, images, lists, forms, other tables, etc.

Table Example

```
<table border="1">
<tr>
<td>row 1, cell 1</td>
<td>row 1, cell 2</td>
</tr>
<tr>
<td>row 2, cell 1</td>
<td>row 2, cell 2</td>
</tr>
</table>
```

This is how the HTML code above will look once translated by a browser. The browser will draw lines around the cells because I included border='1' in the opening <table> tag.

row 1, cell 1	row 1, cell 2
row 2, cell 1	row 2, cell 2

HTML Tables and the Border Attribute

It you do not specify a border attribute, the table will be displayed without borders. Sometimes this can be useful, but most of the time, we want the borders to show.

To display a table without borders, just drop the border attribute:

```
<table>
<tr>
<td>Row 1, cell 1</td>
<td>Row 1, cell 2</td>
</tr>
</table>
```

HTML Table Headers

Headers in a table (the top row which *describes* the data rather than *being* the data) are defined with the <th> tag.

All major browsers display the text in the <th> element as bold and centered.

```
<table border="1">
<tr>
<th>Header 1</th>
<th>Header 2</th>
</tr>
<tr>
<td>row 1, cell 1</td>
<td>row 1, cell 2</td>
</tr>
<tr>
<td>row 2, cell 1</td>
<td>row 2, cell 2</td>
</tr>
</table>
```

How the HTML code above looks in your browser:

Header 1	Header 2
row 1, cell 1	row 1, cell 2
row 2, cell 1	row 2, cell 2

Tables can create accessibility problems. Because tables are inherently meant to be read left to right, one row at a time, using them for layout can cause screen readers to read content out of order and cause confusion for the users who rely on screen readers.

HTML Forms

HTML forms are a special kind of HTML page that can be used to pass data to a server. Once the server gets the data, it may manipulate the data and send some of it back, or it may store it into a database for later use.

An HTML form will contain input elements like labels, text fields, check boxes, radio-select buttons, submit buttons, and more. A form can also present lists, from which the user can make a selection, or a text area where multi-line typing is allowed.

The basic structure of a form is as follows:

```
<form>
.
input elements
.
</form>
```

The form tags go inside the <body> tag. The data in the form is sent to the page specified in the form's action attribute. The file defined in the action attribute usually does something with the received input:

```
<form name="input" action="PostSignup.php" method="get">
```

We'll cover the form actions later.

The Input tag

The most common form element is the <input> element, which is used to collect information from the user. An <input> element has several variations, which depend on the **type** attribute. An <input> element also has a name element, so you can refer to it later. In general, the syntax is:

```
<input type="type" name="name"/>
```

An <input> element can be of type text, checkbox, password, radio button, submit button, and more. The common input types are described.

Text Fields: <input type="text"> defines a one-line input field that a user can enter text into:

```
<form>
First name: <input type="text" name="firstname"/><br>
Last name: <input type="text" name="lastname"/>
</form>
```

This is how the above HTML code would look in a browser:

First name: [_____]
Last name: [_____]

Password Field: <input type="password"> defines a password field. The password field is just like the text field, except the text that is typed in is not displayed on the screen.

```
Password: <input type="password" name="pwd"/>
```

Note that a password field doesn't secure the data, it only hides it on the screen.

Radio Buttons: <input type="radio"> defines a radio button. Radio buttons let a user select one (and only one) of a limited number of presented choices:

```
<body>
<form>
Pick your favorite color: <br/>
<input type="radio" name="color" value="red"/>Red<br/>
```

```
<input type="radio" name="color" value="blue"/>Blue<br/>
<input type="radio" name="color" value="green"/>Green
</form>
</body>
```

This is how the HTML code above looks in a browser:

Pick your favorite color:
○ Red
○ Blue
○ Green

Checkboxes: <input type="checkbox"> defines a checkbox. Checkboxes let a user select ZERO or MORE options of a limited number of choices.

```
<form>
<input type="checkbox" name="vehicle" value="Bike">I have a bike<br>
<input type="checkbox" name="vehicle" value="Car">I have a car
</form>
```

Submit Button: <input type="submit"> defines a submit button.

A submit button is used when the user has filled in the form, and is ready to send ("submit") the data they have entered to the server. The data is sent to the page specified in the form's action attribute, which will be covered in the next section.

HTML Form Actions & Methods

When you define a form, there are two required attributes: action and method. The action attribute (**action=**) indicates the name of the file that the form will be submitted to. The method attribute (**method=**) specifies *how* the form will be submitted.

The file defined in the action attribute usually does something with the received input, like put it into a database or send back some of the values to the user. Here's an example of a simple form with action and method attributes.

```
<form name="input" action="form_action.php" method="get">
Your name: <input type="text" name="name"/>
<input type="submit" value="Submit">
</form>
```

For the purposes of this book we will assume that the action attribute specifies the name of a PHP file. As you will see, the PHP file specified in the action attribute will have access to all the values in the form that was submitted.

We will cover form actions in greater detail in the section *Creating forms to Display, Add, Edit, and Delete data.*

5

Basic PHP Syntax

Introduction - Basic PHP Syntax

A PHP script always starts with **<?php** and ends with **?>**. A PHP script can be placed anywhere inside an HTML document.

```php
<?php
//Imagine some code here ...
?>
```

> In PHP, we use // to make a one-line comment or /* and */ to make a comment block

A PHP file must have a .php extension. A PHP file normally contains HTML tags, and some PHP scripting code. Before we go much further, it is important to note that PHP is case sensitive. Be sure to follow the same casing you see in the examples.

Your first PHP-enabled page – Hello World!

Create a file named hello.php and put it in your web server's root directory (C:\wamp\www?) with the following content:

```
<html>
        <head>
         <title>PHP Test</title>
        </head>
        <body>
         <?php echo '<p>Hello World!</p>'; ?>
        </body>
</html>
```

Use your browser to access the file with your web server's URL, ending with the /hello.php file reference. When developing locally this URL will be something like http://localhost/hello.php or http://127.0.0.1/hello.php but this depends on your computer's configuration.

If everything is configured correctly, this file will be parsed by PHP and magically transformed into HTML. If all goes well, the following HTML will be sent to your browser:

```
<html>
 <head>
        <title>PHP Test</title>
 </head>
 <body>
        <p>Hello World!</p>
 </body>
</html>
```

This program is extremely simple and you really did not need to use PHP to create a page like this. All it does is display "Hello World" using the PHP **echo** statement. However, this is considered the classic way to introduce a programming language – showing users how to say "hello world".

> The PHP echo statement sends whatever text follows the statement to the browser.

Note that there is nothing particularly special about this file. The server knows that this file needs to be interpreted by PHP because you used the ".php" extension, which the server is configured to pass on to PHP. Think of this as a normal HTML file that happens to have a set of special tags available to you that do a lot of interesting things.

The point of the example is to show the special PHP tag format. In this example we used **<?php** to indicate the start of a PHP tag. Then we put the PHP statement and left PHP mode by adding the closing tag, **?>**. You may jump in and out of PHP mode in an HTML file like this anywhere you want.

6

Some Fun Right Away

A Countdown Counter

If you have ever sponsored a project on Kickstarter, you are familiar with the idea of a countdown to a specific date and time. The idea is to create excitement and a sense of urgency. It certainly does for me.

How would you create such a thing in PHP? First we need to set our target date—the time we are counting down to. In the case of the Kickstarter project that launched this book, the target time was 30-September-2012. You can create a variable in PHP to hold the target time by using the mktime (make time) function as follows:

```
$target = mktime(0, 0, 0, 9, 30, 2012) ;
```

mktime
The mktime () function is used to get the timestamp for a specified date. It is phrased as mktime (hour, minute, second, month, day, year, is_dst)

Hour - Number of the hour
Minute - Number of the minute
Second - Number of seconds past the minute
Month - Number of the month
Day - Number of the day
Year - Two or four digit representation of the year. If you use 2 digit 00-69 will be prefixed with 20 (2000-2069) and 70-99 will be prefixed with 19 (1970-1999). If you use 100 it will in interpreted as 2000.
Is_dst - Represents daylight savings time 1=yes, 0=no, and -1= default/unknown.

Next, we need to get the current date. We can do that with this line:

```
$today = time () ;
```

I think you can figure out what the time() function does on your own. :)

Next, we now have to find the difference between the current time and the target time. To do that we simply need to subtract:

```
$difference =($target-$today) ;
```

Since the timestamp is measured in seconds, we need to convert this into whatever units we want. If we want hours we can divide by 3,600, however in our example we will be using days so we need to divide by 86,400 (the number of seconds in a day.) We also want to make sure our number is an integer, so we will use the **int** function.

```
$days =(int) ($difference/86400) ;
```

When we put it all together, we get our final code:

```php
<?php
$target = mktime(0, 0, 0, 2, 10, 2007) ;
$today = time () ;
$difference =($target-$today) ;
$days =(int) ($difference/86400) ;
print "Our event will occur in $days days";
?>
```

Exercise

Build a countdown timer to an event that is significant in your life.

7

Editors and Staying Organized

Editors

An editor is the software you use to write your HTML and code with. For instance, Microsoft Word is the editor that you use to write documents. If you're going to get serious about learning PHP and writing a lot of code, an editor that is specifically designed for PHP will be very helpful.

I use two different editors, depending on what I am focused on. When I am writing HTML, I mostly use Microsoft Expression Web 4. When I am writing PHP code, I use software called phpStorm by JetBrains.

Microsoft Expression Web

What's nice about Expression Web is that it offers a split screen— HTML code on the top and the code as it would be rendered in a browser on the bottom. And you can make edits in either pane, and it automatically updates the other one.

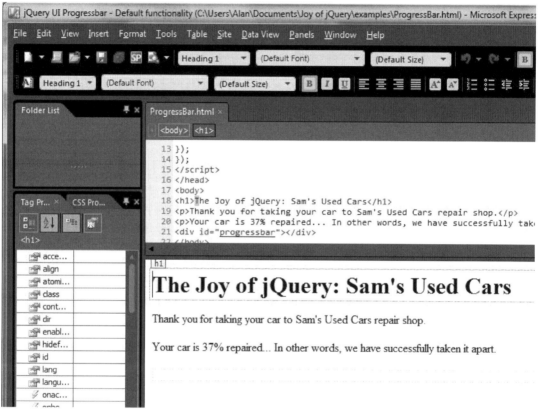

phpStorm

When I am working with PHP code, I use an editor called phpStorm, which is shown below. What's nice about it is that it color-codes PHP text and HTML,

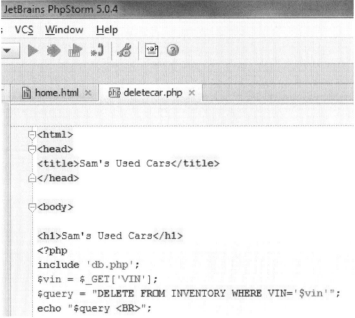

and this makes it much easier to see what you are working on.

EditRocket

Those of you working on Macs will probably like <u>EditRocket</u>

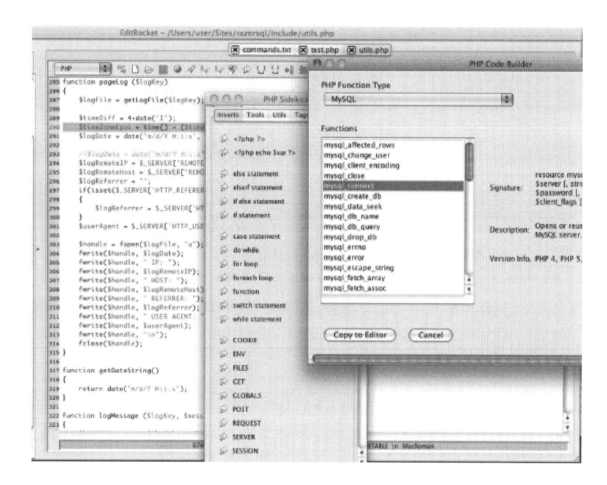

Free Editors

When you are just starting out, it makes sense to start with free editors. Then, if you like working with PHP, it is a lot easier to justify spending money on an editor because you know that you'll use it, and you will have a better sense of what you are looking for.

Programmer's Notepad is a good all purpose editor. Notepad++ is another one.

Dev-PHP is a PHP-specific editor.

TextWrangler is a good editor for the Mac.

Includes

One of the **greatest** features of PHP is the include statement (and the related "require" statement).

What this feature enables is that you can take the parts of a page that would otherwise be repeated over and over in multiple pages and put those parts into a separate file, which you can insert anywhere you would like it just by using the include statement.

Using include files can save a lot of work. For instance, if your web site has a standard header or footer, or if it has a menu for navigation, those elements would likely appear on virtually every page. With ordinary HTML, that means a lot of duplicated code. Duplicated code is fine, until you need to change it— then it becomes a major pain.

With PHP and an include file, you only have to change the file itself, and every page that refers to it will be updated automatically.

> **include** and **require** are virtually identical, except if the specified file cannot be found. **include** will continue with only a warning, but **require** will stop the script dead.
>
> Which to use? It depends if you would *like* to include it, or if you will *require* the file to be included.

Basic example

Assume you have a file called 'top.php' which contains the html that you'd like to appear on the top of several pages. You could easily include it on a page like this:

```
<html>
<body>
<?php include 'top.php'; ?>
<h1>Welcome to Al's Car Wash!</h1>
<p>Some text.</p>
</body>
</html>
```

HTML example

Let's say you have a standard menu that should appear on several pages. Here's the code that makes up the menu:

```
<a href="/default.php">Home</a>
<a href="/products.php">Products</a>
<a href="/services.php">Services</a>
<a href="/about.php">About Us</a>
<a href="/contact.php">Contact Us</a>
```

For every page on which you want the menu, just include the red highlighted text:

```
<html>
<body>
    <div class="leftmenu">
   <?php include 'menu.php'; ?>
</div>

<h1>Welcome to Sam's Used Cars.</h1>
<p>We are glad that you came to visit us today.</p>
```

```
</body>
</html>
```

Code example

Assume we have an include file with some PHP variables defined, and that this file is called ("variables.php"):

```php
<?php
$color='black';
$pet='dog';
?>
```

Then the variables can be used in the calling file:

```php
<html>
<body>

<h1>Welcome to Sam's Used Cars.</h1>
<?php include 'variables.php';
echo "I have a $color $pet"; // I have a black dog
?>

</body>
</html>
```

Best Practices

Using include files is a best practice. The less code you have to repeat, the better. You'll see the sample code that goes along with this book makes extensive use of include statements.

Variables, Numbers, Dates, and Strings

Variables

A variable is a place where you can store things, such as a number, a date, or some text. You put text or numbers into variables so you can retrieve them later or so you can manipulate them. Variables are called variables because the value that they hold can vary. Hence, variables are variable. :) For example, to store the value 3.89 in a variable to track the price of gasoline, the following syntax would apply:

```
$gas_price = 3.89;
```

Storing the price of gas is a good use of a variable because we know the price of gasoline is anything but static! On a different day your variable might contain a different value:

```
$gas_price = 3.79;
```

Although *in theory* you can name your variable just about anything you want, it is a *best practice* to give your variables a name that makes their purpose easy for humans to understand.

For instance, in PHP it would be perfectly OK to name your variables $a, $b, and $c to store information about the color, model, and year of an automobile, doing so would not result in very readable code. See http://www.joyofphp.com/variables-bad-form/

```
<html>
<body>
<h1>Variables</h1>
<?php
echo "<br>";
$a="Ford";
$b="Explorer";
$c = 2003;

echo "This $a $b is a $c <br>";

$gas_price = 3.89;
echo "the price of gas is $gas_price";
?>
</body>
</html>
```

While the code above may be syntactically correct, it is far better to take a moment or two and think about the *purpose* of your variables and name them for their purpose. Compare the above with the following code which has the identical output as the previous code:

```
<html>
<body>
<h1>Variables</h1>
<?php
echo "<br>";
$brand="Ford";
$model="Explorer";
$year = 2003;

echo "This $brand $model is a $year <br>";
```

```
$gas_price = 3.89;
echo "the price of gas is $gas_price";
?>
</body>
</html>
```

See http://www.joyofphp.com/variables-good-form/

Wouldn't you agree that the second style of coding is far easier to read and follow? In a small example like this it doesn't really matter that much, but as you start writing longer and more complex code, naming conventions will make a big difference.

You don't have to declare a variable in PHP prior to using it. The variable will exist as soon as you assign a value to it.

```
$text = "Hello World";
$num = 123;
```

Note that when you assign text to a variable, you put the text in quotes.

Variable Naming Conventions and Best Practices

Variables in PHP are represented by a dollar sign followed by the name of the variable. The variable name is **case-sensitive**, meaning that PHP would treat $price and $Price as two different variables. I can't overemphasize this as a possible source of confusion— variable names are case sensitive, so pay attention.

Variable names follow the same rules as other labels in PHP. A valid variable name starts with a letter or underscore, followed by any number of letters, numbers, or underscores.

Note: **$this** is a special variable that can't be assigned.

When it comes to best practices for naming your variables, there are several ways to do it. One school of thought suggests that every variable and the first word in every variable start with a capital letter, such as $GasPrice. Others would prefer $gas_price. It doesn't really matter which method you select, but what *does* matter is that you are consistent.

Numbers

I think we all know what numbers are. In PHP, you don't have to declare in advance whether a variable will hold a number, string, or date. When you declare a variable and assign a number to it, PHP just knows it is a number. There are many functions you can use to manipulate numbers.

Basic Arithmetic

+ The addition operator

- The subtraction operator; can also be used for negation like this -9

* The multiplication operator

/ The division operator

%, the modulus operator returns the remainder after division. For example, 25 % 3 would give us 1.

You can assign the result of an expression to a variable, and you can use variables in expressions. If you wanted to figure out how much it would cost to fill a tank of gasoline, you might write PHP code like this:

```
$price = 3.79;
$gallons = 10;
$total = $price * $gallons;
echo "The bill for this trip to the gas station is $total";
```

Common Arithmetic Shortcuts

+= adds a value to the current variable. For instance, $a += 1 adds one to the variable $a.

-= subtracts a value from the current variable. For instance, $a -=1 subtracts one from the variable $a.

Useful Numeric Functions

There are many functions related to numbers. Here are a few of the most common and useful:

- **abs()** returns the absolute value of a number

- **pi()** returns the value of pi

- **round()** rounds a number to the nearest integer

- **sqrt()** returns the square root of a number

I think you get the idea. If you need a numeric function, the odds are very high that PHP has that.

Strings

A string is a sequence of characters that are not numbers. In a simpler explanation, it is text. Any combination of letters and spaces can be considered a string. This sentence is a string.

In PHP, it matters if you create a string surrounded by single quotes or double quotes. If you enclose a string within single quotes, PHP will return that exact string. When you enclose a string in double quotes, any variables within the string will be substituted for their values.

```php
<?php
echo 'this is a string';
echo "this is a string";
//both output the same thing
$icecream ="chocolate";
echo 'I like $icecream icecream'; // prints I like $icecream ice cream
echo "I like $icecream icecream"; // prints I like chocolate ice cream
?>
```

Useful String Functions

There is a vast array of functions in PHP that can be used to manipulate string variables. Here are a few:

- **htmlentities()** Converts a string to its HTML equivalent

- **html_entity_decode()** Converts HTML code back to a string

- **str_pad()** Pads a string to a new length

- **str_repeat()**   Repeats a string a specified number of times

- **str_replace()** Replaces some characters in a string (case-sensitive)

- **strtoupper()** converts a string to all upper case

Once again, I think you get the idea. If you need string function, odds are very high that PHP has that.

Sources of Documentation

Two great sources to find specific functions are here:

http://www.w3schools.com

http://www.PHP.net

When you visit PHP.net, at the upper right corner of every page is a search box. Just type the name of a function here, or what you are looking for, and PHP.net will return a list of pages that are relevant.

Exercise

Try searching both PHP.Net and w3schools.com for 'substr'.

How to Interpret PHP.NET documentation

When viewing a functional reference page you need to understand how the syntax is represented in the description, which, in the case of the **substr** function, will look like this:

substr

(PHP 4, PHP 5)

substr — Return part of a string

Description

string **substr** (string $string , int $start [, int $length])

Returns the portion of *string* specified by the *start* and *length* parameters.

This may look like gibberish at first—it certainly did to me. But once you learn to decode it, you'll see that it is actually all that you should need to understand how to use this function. Here's an annotated version:

substr —————— the function name

(PHP 4, PHP 5) —— which versions of PHP have this function

substr — Return part of a string —— What the function does

⊟ **Description**   The function syntax

string **substr** (string *$string* , int *$start* [, int *$length*])

Returns the portion of *string* specified by the *start* and *length* parameters.

The description of what a function does is not always very clear at first, but as you read through the examples that follow, it becomes easier to understand.

The **substr** function can be best thought of as "sub string" or "subset of a string". In general, function names are shortened versions of what they actually do. **substr** lets you extract part of a string.

Let's walk through how to interpret the **function syntax**, shown below again in blue.

string **substr** (string $string , int $start [, int $length])

From left to right:

Return Value

To the left of the function name (substr) is the return value (string).

A return value is what you get back when you run the function. In this case, this function will return a string value. Other functions may return integers, arrays, objects, etc. In some cases, you will see a function return something called bool, which is short for boolean, and this means the function will return either True or False.

If you see a function that returns void, then this means that nothing is returned. "Void" Mixed means that the function can return a mixture of return types like Integer, String, Array, etc.

Function Name

The next part is the name of the function itself. In the blue box above, and on the php.net web site, the name of the function is in bold text.

Parameters

The next part is the parameters passed to the function separated by commas. In each case, there is an example of what type of value that should be passed. In the case of the **Substr** function, the first two parameters are string $string, and int $start. This means you pass the **substr** function a string and an integer. $string is the string you want a subset of, and $start is the position where you want to start looking.

Sometimes you will see a value set within the syntax. This means that this is the default value. In other cases, the parameters are within square brackets. This indicates that the parameter is **optional**, and does not need to be set, but you can use it if you want to.

As you scroll down in the documentation, you will see increasingly obscure uses for a given function. For instance, in the case of **substr**, you can pass negative numbers to either of the number parameters, and it will count from the end of the string, rather than the beginning. Useful? Sure. Common? Not so much.

Here is a simple example use of the **substr** function.

```
$myString = "Hello World";
$myNewString = substr( $myString , 0, 5 );
echo $myNewString;
```

This would print out 'Hello' because the first five characters of 'Hello World' are 'Hello'.

Dates

There is a wide variety of date functions in PHP, with the most obvious one being simply **date()**.

string **date** (string $format, [int $timestamp = time()])

Returns a string formatted according to the given format string using the given integer timestamp or the current time if no timestamp is given. In other words, timestamp is optional and defaults to the value of time().

The date function allows you to format a date in virtually any way you could possibly imagine. The first parameter is the formatting string, which you can build using any combination of the following characters:

format character	Description	Example
Day	—-	—-
d	Day of the month, 2 digits with leading zeros	*01* to *31*
D	A textual representation of a day, three letters	*Mon* through *Sun*
j	Day of the month without leading zeros	*1* to *31*
l (lowercase 'L')	A full textual representation of the day of the week	*Sunday* through *Saturday*
N	ISO-8601 numeric representation of the day of the week (added in PHP 5.1.0)	*1* (for Monday) through *7* (for Sunday)

format character	Description	Example
S	English ordinal suffix for the day of the month, 2 characters	*st*, *nd*, *rd* or *th*. Works well with *j*
w	Numeric representation of the day of the week	*0* (for Sunday) through *6* (for Saturday)
z	The day of the year (starting from 0)	*0* through *365*
Week	—-	—-
W	ISO-8601 week number of year, weeks starting on Monday (added in PHP 4.1.0)	Example: *42* (the 42nd week in the year)
Month	—-	—-
F	A full textual representation of a month, such as January or March	*January* through *December*
m	Numeric representation of a month, with leading zeros	*01* through *12*
M	A short textual representation of a month, three letters	*Jan* through *Dec*
n	Numeric representation of a month, without leading zeros	*1* through *12*
t	Number of days in the given month	*28* through *31*
Year	—-	—-
L	Whether it's a leap year	*1* if it is a leap year, *0* otherwise.

format character	Description	Example
o	ISO-8601 year number. This has the same value as *Y*, except that if the ISO week number (*W*) belongs to the previous or next year, that year is used instead. (added in PHP 5.1.0)	Examples: *1999* or *2003*
Y	A full numeric representation of a year, 4 digits	Examples: *1999* or *2003*
y	A two digit representation of a year	Examples: *99* or *03*
Time	—-	—-
a	Lowercase Ante meridiem and Post meridiem	*am* or *pm*
A	Uppercase Ante meridiem and Post meridiem	*AM* or *PM*
B	Swatch Internet time	*000* through *999*
g	12-hour format of an hour without leading zeros	*1* through *12*
G	24-hour format of an hour without leading zeros	*0* through *23*
h	12-hour format of an hour with leading zeros	*01* through *12*
H	24-hour format of an hour with leading zeros	*00* through *23*
i	Minutes with leading zeros	*00* to *59*
s	Seconds, with leading zeros	*00* through *59*

format character	Description	Example
u	Microseconds (added in PHP 5.2.2). Note that **date()** will always generate *000000* since it takes an integer parameter, whereas DateTime::format() does support microseconds.	Example: *654321*
Timezone	—-	—-
e	Timezone identifier (added in PHP 5.1.0)	Examples: *UTC, GMT, Atlantic/Azores*
I (capital i)	Whether or not the date is in daylight saving time	*1* if Daylight Saving Time, *0* otherwise.
O	Difference to Greenwich time (GMT) in hours	Example: *+0200*
P	Difference to Greenwich time (GMT) with colon between hours and minutes (added in PHP 5.1.3)	Example: *+02:00*
T	Timezone abbreviation	Examples: *EST, MDT ...*
Z	Timezone offset in seconds. The offset for timezones west of UTC is always negative, and for those east of UTC is always positive.	*-43200* through *50400*
Full Date/Time	—-	—-
c	ISO 8601 date (added in PHP 5)	2004-02-12T15:19:21+00:00

format character	Description	Example
r	» RFC 2822 formatted date	Example: *Thu, 21 Dec 2000 16:01:07 +0200*
U	Seconds since the Unix Epoch (January 1 1970 00:00:00 GMT)	See also time()

Unrecognized characters in the format string will be printed as-is. The *Z* format will always return *0* when using gmdate().

Example: Calculating Age in Years

Assuming that as part of a registration procedure you asked for a birthday, this function will return their age in years.

```php
<?php

//calculate years of age (input string: YYYY-MM-DD)
function age($age){
list($year,$month,$day) = explode("-",$age);
$year_diff = date("Y") - $year;
$month_diff = date("m") - $month;
$day_diff  = date("d") - $day;
if ($day_diff < 0 || $month_diff < 0)
 $year_diff—;
return $year_diff;
}

?>
```

See the example script AgeInYears.php

Variable Scope

The scope of a variable defines where the value can be accessed. If a variable is declared on its own line on a page, it is available anywhere on that page. If a variable is declared within a function, it will only be available within that function.

If you want a particular variable to be available everywhere, declare it using the global keyword, such as

global $a = 'Hello';

There is a special kind of variable that can be accessed on **every page** that makes up your web application. This topic is covered in *Session Variables.*

Control Structures

Introduction

The whole point of PHP is to make a web page dynamic. Dynamic means that you don't *necessarily* get the same result when you view the same page from time to time. Sometimes the web page will display one group of text, and other times it will display another group. Control structures allow you to control the conditions that specify the rules that define when and how this happens.

if

The **if** statement is one of the most important features of many languages, PHP included. It allows for conditional execution of code fragments. In PHP, the simple form of the **if** statement is as follows

```
if (expression)
  statement
```

The expression is evaluated to its boolean value. If expression evaluates to TRUE, PHP will execute statement, and if it evaluates to FALSE – PHP will ignore it.

> A **Boolean** value is one that can be reduced to one of two values: True or False

If you would like to execute multiple statements if the condition is true, then group the statements within a code block using the curly braces, as shown

```
if (expression)
{
    statement 1;
    statement 2;
}
```

The following example would display 'a is bigger than b' **if** $a is bigger than $b:

```php
<?php
if ($a > $b)
 echo "a is bigger than b";
?>
```

if... else

Often you will want to execute a statement *if* a certain condition **is met**, and a different statement *if* the condition is **not met**. This is what the **else** statement is for—for defining the action if the condition is not met.

More formally, **else** *extends* an if statement to execute a statement in case the expression in the if statement evaluates to FALSE.

For example, if today is Monday the store is closed. Otherwise it is open from 10 AM to 9 PM. The function <u>date_default_timezone_set</u> defines which time zone to use.

```
<html>
<body>
<h1>Open Hours</h1>
<?php
date_default_timezone_set ( "EST" );
if ( date("l")=='Sunday') {
                echo "Sorry, we are closed today.";
} else {
        echo "We are open today from 10 AM to 9 PM";
}
?>
</body>
</html>
```

Exercise: Open Hours

Let's assume that you run a store of some kind (a gym, a donut shop, a farm stand, used car lot, whatever), and the hours it is open vary each day. Saturdays and Sundays are the busiest days, so it is open from 9 AM – 9 PM. Monday is your day off, and the rest of the week the hours are 10 AM – 6 PM, except in the summer (July and August) when you stay open until 7 PM.

You would like the home page of your web site to prominently display Today's Hours, similar to the screen shot below:

PHP Switch

The switch statement is similar to a series of IF statements on the same expression. On many occasions, you may want to compare the same variable (or expression) with many different values, and execute a different piece of code depending on which value it equals to. This is what the switch statement is for.

```php
<?php
switch ($make) {
 case "Ford":
  echo "Your car is a Ford";
  break;
 case "Chevrolet":
  echo "Your car is a Chevrolet";
  break;
 case "Toyota":
  echo "Your car is a Toyota";
```

```
    break;
}
?>
```

PHP Looping

PHP while

The **while** loop is one of the simplest type of loop in PHP. Basically, it continues to do something as long as a condition is true.

The basic syntax of a while loop is as follows:

```
while (expression){
  do something;
  do something else;
}
```

Here's an example:

```
<?php
$i = 1;
while ($i <= 10):
  echo $i;
  $i++;
endwhile;
?>
```

This code would print out the numbers 1 to 10. A common use of a while loop is to continue to print something as long as you had database records to process.

PHP for

For loops are a bit more complex. The syntax for a for loop is as follows:

```
for (expression1; expression2; expression3) {
   statement;
   statement;
}
```

The first expression (expression1) is executed once, no matter what, at the beginning of the loop.

At the **beginning** of each iteration through the loop, expression2 is evaluated. If expression2 evaluates to TRUE, the loop continues and the nested statement(s) are executed. If it evaluates to FALSE, the execution of the loop ends.

At the **end** of each iteration, which is to say after all the statements have been executed, expression3 is executed.

Consider the following example, which also displays the numbers 1 through 10:

```
for ($i = 1; $i <= 10; $i++) {
  echo $i.'<br>';
}
```

Here's how it works. Expression1 assigns $i the value of 1. This happens no matter what. Expression2 tests to see if $i is less than 10. Since 1 is less than 10, PHP executes the statements that follow. If $i was not less than 10, none of the statements would have executed. In this case there is only one statement, which is echo $i.'
'. After the statement(s) have executed, it executes expression3, which increments $i by one. Now $i is 2, which is less than 10, so it echoes 2, and so on.

10

How to use a database, specifically mySQL

Introduction

Sure the idea of dynamic web pages is cool, but you can only go far with what's built into PHP, like changing the page based on the day of the week. What you'd really like to do is make a web page unique for each visitor, and that's where databases come in.

We will begin this chapter assuming that the reader has absolutely no knowledge of MySQL or databases. First, we'll explain databases, then we'll create one the easy way— using phpMyAdmin. Then we'll cover how to create databases and tables using SQL, and in the next chapter we'll show how all this can be done using PHP.

What are Databases?

Let's begin our tutorial with an introduction to our test subject, Sam, who runs a used car dealership. When he first started his business, he only had a few cars— so keeping track of them was pretty easy. But after a while, his dealership began to grow. Soon he had 10 cars on his lot, and a year later he had 25 cars.

Every car has a number of unique attributes to track, such make, model, color, year, VIN, number of passengers, body style, MPG, acquisition cost, asking price, etc. As you can imagine, at some point a human just can't keep track of all that information, and even if *Sam* could keep it all straight, he also needs to convey that information to his sales people, who don't always have the same passion for Sam's business that Sam has. So Sam needs the ability to quickly print out a "Cheat Sheet" for each car that a sales person can refer to when a prospect wanders onto the car lot.

And of course, Sam would really like to have a web site that allows people to **search** for the type of car they want to see if he has any candidates, and to **browse** all the available cars that he has—which, of course, is always changing.

Because the inventory of cars is always changing, a static web site isn't going to be the solution. A database-based web site is the solution.

Databases help to organize and track things. Databases allow you to use creativity to group things together in meaningful ways, and to present the same set of information in different ways to different audiences.

> "Databases" are simply an organized collection of data stored in a computer.

Databases are composed of one or more "tables". Tables are composed of parts called "rows" and "columns" similar to what you would see in a spreadsheet. The columns section of each table declares the characteristics of each table while each row contains unique data for each element in the table.

It may sound complicated but actually it is quite simple. Take the example below which is one way that Sam could begin to organize his car collection. (Note that for brevity, not all possible car attributes are shown.)

Table: Cars

ID	VIN	Make	Model	Style	Year	Price
1	1328237824	Ford	Explorer	SUV	2005	5995
2	4797834923	Dodge	RAM	Pickup	2008	7200
3	2394923724	Mazda	6	Passenger	2010	9995
4	2342323634	Subaru	Outback	Passenger	2007	4500

We can clearly see that the elements in this table has seven **columns** defined as ID, VIN, Make, Model, Style, Year, and Price. The table has four **rows** that describe four different cars— a Ford Explorer, Dodge RAM, Mazda 6, and a Subaru Outback.

Here is a quick review of what we have learned.

- **Tables** are just a collection of things that you want to keep track of.

- **Tables** consist of rows and columns.

- **Columns** hold the different attributes of each element in that table. Rows in a table hold different instances uniquely defined by the table's columns.

- **Databases** are a collection of tables.

Getting Started with phpMyAdmin

Recall from the section *How Do I Know it is Working* on page 22 that if you navigate to http://localhost you will see a page that was created by your local server. In my case it is WAMPSERVER.

At the bottom of the page you should see a link for **Your Aliases**

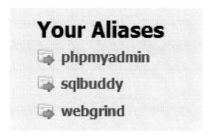

I am not sure if Macs see this, but if you don't see the link, just enter this address into your browser or click on this link: http://localhost/phpmyadmin/

Clicking that link should take you to a page that is similar to this:

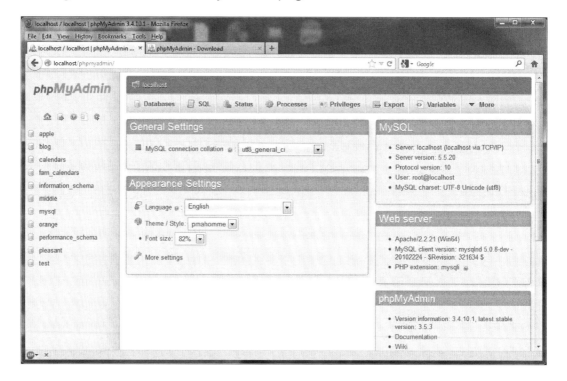

What is phpMyAdmin?

phpMyAdmin is a free software tool—that just happens to be written in PHP itself— that is intended to handle many common administration task of MySQL using a browser. phpMyAdmin supports a wide range of operations with MySQL. The most frequently used operations are supported by the user interface (managing databases, tables, fields, relations, indexes, users, permissions, etc), and you still have the ability to directly execute a SQL statement if you prefer.

phpMyAdmin comes with a good supply of documentation and users are welcome to update the wiki pages to share ideas and feedback. The phpMyAdmin team will try to help you if you face any problem, but I haven't personally had any problems with it. What it does, it does well.

Using phpMyAdmin to create a database

First navigate such that you have phpMyAdmin on the screen. Click on the link that says Databases:

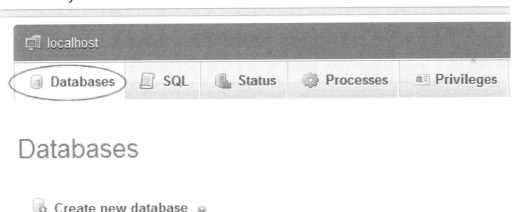

In the box that says Create new database, type the word 'Cars', then click on the Create button. If it worked properly, you should see a yellow confirmation box appear on the screen briefly, as below:

Introduction to SQL

This is equivalent to issuing the SQL command

CREATE DATABASE Cars;

and, in fact, phpMyAdmin actually executed that **exact** SQL command in the background for you when you clicked on the button. In other words, you can think of phpMyAdmin as a tool that builds SQL commands for you.

SQL (pronounced "sequel") or Structured Query Language) is a language all its own. SQL is a special-purpose programming language designed for managing data in relational database management systems, such as mySQL. SQL can be used to create databases, create tables, and insert, update, and delete data into tables.

Using phpMyAdmin to create a Table in a database

Now that the database is created, we would like to use it. Find the cars database in the list of databases, then click on the database name.

Databases

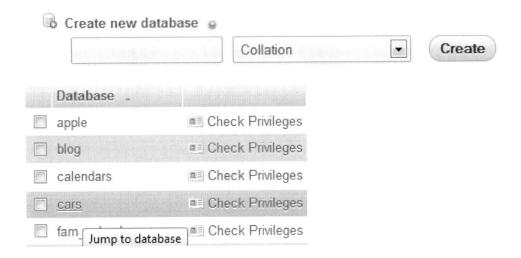

phpMyAdmin will provide a page similar to:

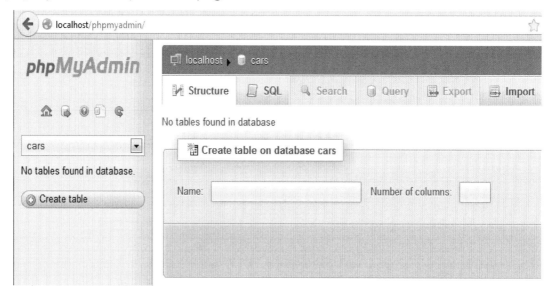

This is the equivalent to the SQL command:

USE cars;

This tells the MySQL database that you are going to work in the database *cars* until you say otherwise.

You have just created the database for our fictional used car lot. We will develop this database more as we go along.

Defining our first table

So far, you have created your database, and figured out the general structure of PHPMyAdmin. Now you will need to put a table inside of the database you have created. In the case of our cars database, we will need to define the table to describe the cars and trucks that Sam has for sale on his used car lot.

Here's a screen shot that I took from www.cars.com that describes a car.

Features:

Price: 8995
Model:**Explorer** Eddie Bauer
Mileage: 90832
Exterior Color: Red Fire Metallic
Body Style: Sport Utility
Stock Number: cb232

Make: Ford
Year:2004
Condition: Used
Interior Color: Med Parchment
Transmission: 5-SPEED AUTOMATIC
Vin Number: 1FMZU74K94UB86311

Before creating **your** table, think about what you are going to put into the table and what are the various attributes that might distinguish one row (car) from another for your application?

What defines an automobile?

I can think of a number of properties or attributes that distinguish one car from another on a used car lot.

- Vehicle ID Number (VIN)
- Year
- Make
- Model
- Trim
- Exterior color
- Interior color
- Asking Price
- Purchase Price
- Mileage
- Transmission
- Purchase Date
- Sale Date
- Sale Price

That should be enough to at least let us get started. Now we have to figure out what kind of data we are going to put in these categories.

Datatypes

For learning purposes, there are really only three types of data you will need to use. They are:

1. Numbers
2. Characters
3. Dates

Numbers

Numbers, as the name probably gives away, are any kind of numeric information. Will you need to use any kind of decimals for the data that you are going to store? In that case, you will need to use the datatype decimal or float. If not, you can use the datatype int (short for integer) or bigint (a big integer—which takes up more space, but can handle bigger numbers).

Characters

The character type in MySQL is the data type you use to store Strings. Characters are used to store the representation of a letter, word, or series of words. For example the letter A and the phrase 'Hello World' would both be of a character type. MySQL calls this a VARCHAR, short for variable characters. It is variable because you only set the maximum number of characters that the field can hold, and if you put in a value with fewer characters, the shorter value will be stored. Other databases, such as Microsoft SQL Server, offer the CHAR datatype, which will fill in any unused characters with spaces. Why anyone would want that I can't imagine, so for simplicity we'll stick to VARCHAR for now.

Use the datatype varchar(n) to define a column that you would like to represent with a character. Substitute the n in varchar(n) with the maximum amount of letters a column in your table can have (up to 255). Spaces, tabs, and newlines in a paragraph all count as characters.

Dates

Dates are a way to store dates in the database. Do you just want to store the date and not the time? Use the datatype date. Do you want to store the time and not the date? Use the datatype time. Want to store the date and the time? Use the datatype datetime.

Let's look back at our characteristics of cars to decide what kind of datatype they should be.

- Year - Consists of numbers without a decimal point. Int
- Make – Consists of text. Varchar(25)
- Vehicle ID Number (VIN) – Varchar(17)
- Model – Consists of text and the occasional number. Varchar(25)
- Trim – Consists of text. Varchar(25)
- Exterior color – Consists of text. Varchar(25)
- Interior color – Consists of text. Varchar(25)
- Asking Price - Consists of numbers with decimal point. Decimal
- Purchase Price - Consists of numbers with a decimal point. Decimal
- Mileage - Consists of numbers without a decimal point. Int
- Transmission – Consists of text. Varchar(25)
- Purchase (Acquisition) Date - Date
- Sale Date - Date
- Sale Price - Consists of numbers without a decimal point. Int

That about sums up the table that we need to create to track our cars. Since the VIN is the only truly unique element in the list, we will make this the "Primary Key".

Defining a column as a primary key means that the column will only be able to have unique values (i.e. nothing can repeat itself). In the case of this specific table, it means that you can't enter two cars with the same VIN into the database, because we have just told mySQL that this isn't allowed. Some examples of this in everyday life are license plate numbers, credit card numbers, and social security numbers. All of these cases work to make sure that each instance is unique. The same concept applies to tables in databases. Whenever possible, it is good practice to make sure that the table you are creating contains some form of primary key, to give something to uniquely identify a row.

How do I make a table with this information? Great question. Although we created the *database* using the phpMyAdmin wizard, from now on we're just going to use SQL.

In your window with phpMyAdmin, make sure that the cars table is selected (see it circled in red below) then click on the SQL tab to bring up the command box .

Make sure that you see localhost -> cars above the box. If you do not, just click on the cars link on the right side and then the SQL tab to get yourself there.

Type the following command into the box and click go.

CREATE TABLE INVENTORY (VIN varchar(17) PRIMARY KEY, YEAR INT, Make varchar(50), Model varchar(100), TRIM varchar(50), EXT_COLOR varchar (50), INT_COLOR varchar (50), ASKING_PRICE DECIMAL (10,2), SALE_PRICE DECIMAL (10,2), PURCHASE_PRICE DECIMAL (10,2), MILEAGE int, TRANSMISSION varchar (50), PURCHASE_DATE DATE, SALE_DATE DATE)

Congratulations! You have created the INVENTORY table.

Here's an incredibly useful tip: Click the link "**Create PHP Code**" located on the right side of the screen as shown in the following screen shot:

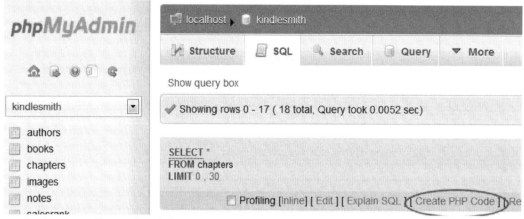

and what you'll get back is:

```
$sql = " CREATE TABLE INVENTORY ( VIN varchar(17) PRIMARY KEY, YEAR INT, Make varchar(50), Model varchar(100), TRIM varchar(50), EXT_COLOR varchar (50), INT_COLOR varchar (50), ASKING_PRICE DECIMAL (10,2), SALE_PRICE DECIMAL (10,2), PURCHASE_PRICE DECIMAL (10,2), MILEAGE int, TRANSMISSION varchar (50), PURCHASE_DATE DATE, SALE_DATE DATE)";
```

The reason there is such a link is because anything **you can do** in mySQL using a SQL command, you can tell PHP to do for you **in code**. This represents a valid line of PHP code in which the variable **$sql** is assigned a string value to hold the SQL statement. Of course, there is more that would need to be done beyond this single line of code, but don't worry— we will cover this shortly.

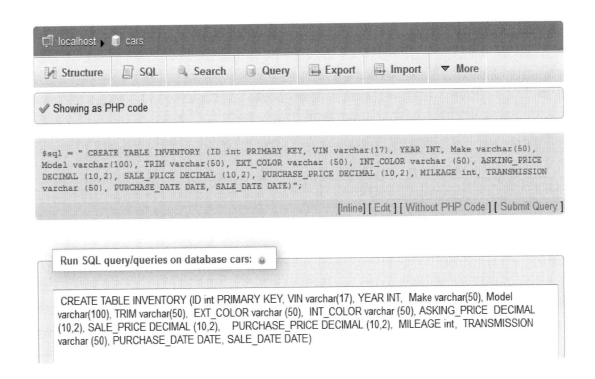

Exercise: Create a Table

Create a table using a SQL statement, then delete the table and create it again using phpMyAdmin . Which is easier? phpMyAdmin is your friend!

Working with SQL Statements

INSERT Statements

Now that you have a table created, the next logical step is to put some data into our table. In the world of SQL, this is accomplished with the INSERT command.

> The syntax for inserting into a table is as follows:
>
> INSERT INTO {Name of table} (Column Names) VALUES (Column Values);

Click on the SQL tab again, type the following command (if you can), and press enter.

```
INSERT INTO `cars`.`inventory` (`VIN`, `YEAR`, `Make`, `Model`, `TRIM`, `EXT_COLOR`,
`INT_COLOR`, `ASKING_PRICE`, `SALE_PRICE`, `PURCHASE_PRICE`, `MILEAGE`,
`TRANSMISSION`, `PURCHASE_DATE`, `SALE_DATE`) VALUES (' 5FNYF4H91CB054036', '2012',
'Honda', 'Pilot', 'Touring', 'White Diamond Pearl', 'Leather', '37807', NULL, '34250', '7076',
'Automatic', '2012-11-08', NULL);
```

Obviously, writing SQL isn't *conceptually* difficult... but it is tedious and prone to error, especially as the statement gets longer.   This statement:

```
INSERT INTO `cars`.`inventory` ( `YEAR`, `Make`, `Model`, `ASKING_PRICE`) VALUES ( '2012',
'Honda', 'Pilot', '37807');
```

is pretty easy to follow, but this next one is a bit tougher:

```
INSERT INTO `cars`.`inventory` (`VIN`, `YEAR`, `Make`, `Model`, `TRIM`, `EXT_COLOR`,
`INT_COLOR`, `ASKING_PRICE`, `SALE_PRICE`, `PURCHASE_PRICE`, `MILEAGE`,
`TRANSMISSION`, `PURCHASE_DATE`, `SALE_DATE`) VALUES (' 5FNYF4H91CB054036', '2012',
'Honda', 'Pilot', 'Touring', 'White Diamond Pearl', 'Leather', '37807', NULL, '34250', '7076',
'Automatic', '2012-11-08', NULL);
```

The only difference is the number of fields. The syntax is the same, but the challenge becomes making sure that there is a one-to-one relationship for each column name and value, and that they are in the right order— the column names and their respective values, that is.

As you can see, writing an INSERT statement is easy to goof up. We all do it. Luckily, phpMyAdmin makes it easy to generate perfect SQL statements. Simply click on the table, then click the **Insert** button and enter values into the boxes, as shown:

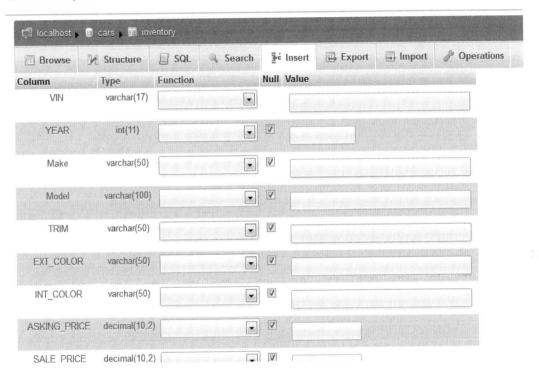

Once you click the **Go** button, phpMyAdmin will create a SQL statement for you and insert the record, and even offer to convert it into a line of PHP code for you.

Here's a trick used by the professionals: once you have one line of SQL that works, it's pretty easy to copy and paste then tweak the values for the next car. Go ahead and enter some more values until you get 5 or 6 cars entered into your table. Here's another one:

```
INSERT INTO `cars`.`inventory` (`VIN`, `YEAR`, `Make`, `Model`, `TRIM`, `EXT_COLOR`, `INT_COLOR`, `ASKING_PRICE`, `SALE_PRICE`, `PURCHASE_PRICE`, `MILEAGE`, `TRANSMISSION`, `PURCHASE_DATE`, `SALE_DATE`) VALUES ('  4T4BF3EK5AR031954', '2010', 'Toyota', 'Camry', 'LE', ' Magnetic Gray Metallic', 'Tan cloth', '16977', NULL, '14250', ' 32673', '6 Speed Automatic', '2012-11-08', NULL);
```

Don't worry if you mess up. MySQL will warn you, and prevent you from running incorrect commands. You don't need to enter 10 or 20 cars as the sample code includes a script that does that for you. Just do it enough times that you get it.

SELECT Statements

The syntax of SQL is pretty straight forward, at least syntactically. We have used it thus far to create a database, create a table within that database, and insert data into the table.

There are just a few basic transactions left for us to master: reading data, updating data, and deleting data. Some people refer to this with the cheery acronym CRUD, for Create, Read, Update, and Delete.

Reading data is accomplished using the SELECT statement. The SELECT statement selects a value or group of values from a table and returns those value(s) to the user. Here's an easy way to remember it: The SELECT statement allows you to be selective. Clever, eh?

> The syntax for selecting data from a table is as follows:
>
> SELECT (Column Names) FROM (Table Name);

Let's start out with a simple SELECT statement. In phpMyAdmin, click on the cars icon on the left side and then click on the SQL tab at the top of the page. Type in the following command and press Go.

SELECT * FROM inventory;

In general, the asterisk character (*) in computer lingo is called a wildcard and basically means "everything", so the result of the command above should return all rows and columns of the inventory table, and look similar to:

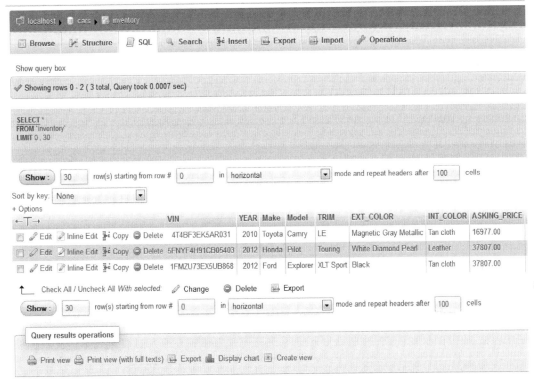

If you typed out this statement correctly, you should see the *entire* contents of your table 'inventory'. To select only *certain* columns of a table, type out all of the columns you want to see in that table separated by a comma. Type in the following command and press Go.

SELECT `Make`, `Model`, `ASKING_PRICE`FROM `inventory`

You should see something like this:

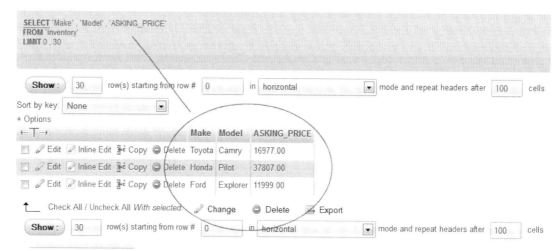

Note that I added the red circle and line to show you where to look. The mySQL database only returned the columns you specified using the SELECT statement.

WHERE Statements

So far, you have learned how to get **all** the rows and columns from a table, and how to get **selected columns** from a table, but what about **selected rows**?

This is where the **WHERE** statement comes into play. The WHERE statement gives a specific set of criteria to the MySQL database so that the results are much more controlled and relevant to what you want. For example, say that you want to select all the Ford Explorers that are in the inventory, or all the Toyotas under $15,000. The WHERE clause makes this possible.

SELECT `Model`, `TRIM`, `EXT_COLOR` FROM inventory WHERE Make = 'Ford'

The results should be every automobile made by Ford in the database. If you wanted just Ford Explorers, you would need to have WHERE Make='Ford' AND Model = 'Explorer.

Of course, if you were looking to buy a car, you would only be interested in those cars that haven't already been sold, so the following query might be better suited:

```
SELECT `Model`, `TRIM`, `EXT_COLOR` FROM inventory WHERE Make = 'Toyota' AND
`SALE_DATE` IS Null
```

NULL is a special word meaning that the field does not contain a value, and for some reason you can't say **= NULL**, you have to say **IS NULL**. I'm sure there is a reason for this, but it doesn't really matter. It is what it is.

Comparison Operators

There are many different comparison operators in addition to = and IS.

Operation	Symbol
Equal To	=
Not Equal To	!=
Greater Than	>
Less Than	<
Greater Than Or Equal To	>=
Less Than Or Equal To	<=

Remember to surround a string with quotations or parentheses every time you wish to use them in SQL statements. They will not work otherwise. Also, the WHERE command always goes **after** the SELECT statement in MySQL.

To find all of the automobiles with a year that is a 2010 or newer, it is fairly obvious that we need to use the **Greater Than Or Equal To** operator defined above. Type the following command into your compiler and press Go.

```
SELECT `Make`, `Mode`, `EXT_COLOR` FROM inventory WHERE YEAR > = 2010 AND
`SALE_DATE` IS Null
```

ORDER BY

The ORDER BY statement is probably one of the easiest and handiest commands in SQL. You can attach it at the end of any SELECT statement to put the results in the order of the column that you specify.

```
SELECT * FROM inventory ORDER BY YEAR DESC
```

The above statement should display the automobiles in order of the column 'Year' with the newest cars at the top. This is because the modifier DESC, or descending, is placed at the end of the command.

```
SELECT * FROM inventory WHERE YEAR > = 2006 ORDER BY YEAR ASC
```

The above statement should display the automobiles in order of the column 'Year' with the oldest cars at the top. This is because the modifier ASC, or ascending, is placed at the end of the command.

The ORDER BY modifier can also be used with a WHERE statement such as:

```
SELECT * FROM inventory WHERE YEAR > = 2006 ORDER BY YEAR ASC
```

Just remember that the **WHERE** command always goes **before** the **ORDER BY** command. If you mix them up, you will get an error.

To limit how many results you receive in an ORDER BY statement, use the limit clause after you write 'asc' or 'desc', such as

```
SELECT * FROM inventory ORDER BY YEAR DESC limit 10;
```

The number after limit determines how many results are returned.

UPDATE Statements

To update existing records in a database, you use the UPDATE statement. This would be useful, for example, when a car in the inventory goes on sale with a lower asking price.

The syntax for an update statement is

```
UPDATE table_name

SET column1=value, column2=value2,...

WHERE some_column=some_value
```

To change the asking price for a car in our database, you can use a statement such as:

```
UPDATE `cars`.`inventory` SET `ASKING_PRICE` = '36999' WHERE `inventory`.`VIN` = '5FNYF4H91CB054036';
```

DELETE Statements

To delete records from a database you use the **DELETE** statement, specifying the table name and a WHERE clause that specifies which records to delete.

```
DELETE FROM table_name

WHERE some_column=some_value
```

For example, to delete the Caravan cars from the inventory you could use a command similar to

```
DELETE from inventory WHERE `Model` = 'Caravan'
```

If you wanted to delete everything from a database table, you could skip the WHERE clause and use our friend the wildcard with a statement like

```
DELETE * from inventory
```

11

Using mySQL and PHP Together

Introduction

In the previous chapter, we learned all the basics of using a database, in our case mySQL. All the SQL statements that we learned so far would likely work with other database systems, such as Microsoft SQL Server. In general, common SQL commands work across all databases. Occasionally you'll find minor differences, but other database systems are beyond the scope of this book.

Thus far we created our SQL statements either by hand, mostly, or with the aid of phpmyAdmin. In this chapter, we're going to use PHP and mySQL together. This is where it really starts to get good.

Code!

The PHP code listing that follows will automate all the steps we covered in the prior chapter to create a database, create a table, and insert records into the table.

If it all works as intended, you should see a screen like this:

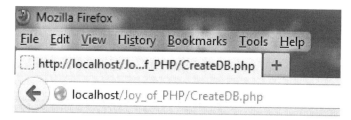

Connected successfully to mySQL.

Database Cars created

Database table 'INVENTORY' created

Honda Pilot inserted into inventory table.

Dodge Durango inserted into inventory table.

The code that follows is numbered for the convenience of explaining it, but remember that you can get the sample code from the website, http://www.joyofphp.com. This particular script is called 'createdb.php'.

You don't need to study every line as it is presented here. Just give it a quick look over. In the next section, I will go over the entire script line by line and explain each one.

Code Listing: createdb.php

```
1.<?php
2./**
3. * Joy of PHP sample code
4. * Demonstrates how to create a database, create a table, and insert records.
5. */
6.
7.$mysqli = new mysqli('localhost', 'root', 'mypassword' );
8.
9. if (!$mysqli) {
10.   die('Could not connect: ' . mysql_error());
11. }
```

```
12. echo 'Connected successfully to mySQL. <BR>';
13.
14.
15./* Create table doesn't return a resultset */
16.if ($mysqli->query("CREATE DATABASE Cars") === TRUE) {
17.  echo "<p>Database Cars created</P>";
18.}
19.else
20.{
21.  echo "Error creating Cars database: " . mysql_error()."<br>";
22.}
23.//select a database to work with
24.$mysqli->select_db("Cars");
25. Echo ("Selected the Cars database");
26.
27.$query = " CREATE TABLE INVENTORY
28.( VIN varchar(17) PRIMARY KEY, YEAR INT, Make varchar(50), Model varchar(100),
29.TRIM varchar(50), EXT_COLOR varchar (50), INT_COLOR varchar (50), ASKING_PRICE DECIMAL (10,2),
30.SALE_PRICE DECIMAL (10,2), PURCHASE_PRICE DECIMAL (10,2), MILEAGE int,
TRANSMISSION varchar (50), PURCHASE_DATE DATE, SALE_DATE DATE)";
31.//echo "<p>***********</p>";
32.//echo $query ;
33.//echo "<p>***********</p>";
34.if ($mysqli->query($query) === TRUE)
35.{
36.  echo "Database table 'INVENTORY' created</P>";
37.}
38.else
39.{
40.  echo "<p>Error: </p>" . mysql_error();
41.}
42.// Dates are stored in MySQL as 'YYYY-MM-DD' format
43.$query = "INSERT INTO `cars`.`inventory`
44.(`VIN`, `YEAR`, `Make`, `Model`, `TRIM`, `EXT_COLOR`, `INT_COLOR`, `ASKING_PRICE`,
`SALE_PRICE`, `PURCHASE_PRICE`, `MILEAGE`, `TRANSMISSION`, `PURCHASE_DATE`,
`SALE_DATE`)
45.VALUES
46.('5FNYF4H91CB054036', '2012', 'Honda', 'Pilot', 'Touring', 'White Diamond Pearl', 'Leather',
```

```php
'37807', NULL, '34250', '7076', 'Automatic', '2012-11-08', NULL);";
47.
48.
49.if ($mysqli->query($query) === TRUE) {
50.  echo "<p>Honda Pilot inserted into inventory table. </p>";
51.}
52.else
53.{
54.  echo "<p>Error inserting Honda Pilot: </p>" . mysql_error();
55.  echo "<p>***********</p>";
56.  echo $query ;
57.  echo "<p>***********</p>";
58.}
59.
60.// Insert a Dodge Durango
61.
62.$query = "INSERT INTO `cars`.`inventory` (`VIN`, `YEAR`, `Make`, `Model`, `TRIM`,
`EXT_COLOR`, `INT_COLOR`, `ASKING_PRICE`, `SALE_PRICE`, `PURCHASE_PRICE`, `MILEAGE`,
`TRANSMISSION`, `PURCHASE_DATE`, `SALE_DATE`)
63.VALUES
64.('LAKSDFJ234LASKRF2', '2009', 'Dodge', 'Durango', 'SLT', 'Silver', 'Black', '2700', NULL,
'2000', '144000', '4WD Automatic', '2012-12-05', NULL);";
65.
66.If ($mysqli->query($query) === TRUE) {
67.  echo "<p>Dodge Durango inserted into inventory table.</p>";
68.}
69.else
70.{
71.  echo "<p>Error Inserting Dodge: </p>" . mysql_error();
72.  echo "<p>***********</p>";
73.  echo $query ;
74.  echo "<p>***********</p>";
75.}
76.
77.
78.$mysqli->close();
79.?>
```

Code Explained: createdb.php

Next I'll walk you through the code, line by line. Please take the time to follow along with me, as this is the **only way** to really get it. Yes, every line *does* matter.

```
1.<?php
```

line 1 is the start tag for PHP, and it tells the PHP interpreter that what follows is code, not HTML.

```
2. /**
3.  * Joy of PHP sample code
4.  * Demonstrates how to create a database, create a table, and insert records.
5.  */
```

lines 2 - 5 are comments. Comments are good, so put lots of comments in your code.

```
7. $mysqli = new mysqli('localhost', 'root', 'mypassword' );
```

line 7 creates a variable called $con (for connection) and sets it equal to a built-in function for connecting to mySQL. You need to supply the hostname, username, and password for your mySQL server. If you do not have the correct username and password, you will see this:

Could not connect: Access denied for user 'root'@'localhost' (using password: YES)

```
9. if (!$mysqli) {
```

line 9 is the start of an **if** statement, saying basically "if you are not connected". The point of this line is to test to see if line 7 succeeded.

```
10.  die('Could not connect: ' . mysql_error());
```

line 10 is what to do if the connection failed. **'die'** is a command that stops further code execution and prints out the text that follows. If I had been the one who invented PHP, I might have named that command 'stop' rather than 'die', but it does make the point.

```
12. echo 'Connected successfully to mySQL. <BR>';
```

line 12 prints out "Connected successfully to mySQL". This is the first line you see in the browser.

```
16. if ($mysqli->query("CREATE DATABASE Cars") === TRUE) {
17.  echo "<p>Database Cars created</P>";
18. }
19. else
20. {
21.  echo "Error creating Cars database: " . mysql_error()."<br>";
22. }
```

line 16 tests for the execution of the SQL statement "Create Database Cars" using the connection created in line 7.

line 17 prints to the browser if the SQL statement in line 15 ran without error.

line 21 prints error information to the browser if the SQL statement in line 15 did not run successfully.

```
23. //select a database to work with
```

line 23 is a comment. Comments are good.

```
24. $mysqli->select_db("Cars");
```

line 24 creates a variable called $selected which uses a built-in function for selecting a mySQL database, using the connection created in line 7.

```
25. Echo ("Selected the Cars database");
```

line 25 prints "Selected the Cars database" to the browser.

```
27. $query = " CREATE TABLE INVENTORY
28. ( VIN varchar(17) PRIMARY KEY, YEAR INT, Make varchar(50), Model varchar(100),
29. TRIM varchar(50), EXT_COLOR varchar (50), INT_COLOR varchar (50), ASKING_PRICE
DECIMAL (10,2),
30. SALE_PRICE DECIMAL (10,2), PURCHASE_PRICE DECIMAL (10,2), MILEAGE int,
TRANSMISSION varchar (50), PURCHASE_DATE DATE, SALE_DATE DATE)";
```

lines 27 - 30 creates a variable called $query which holds a SQL statement. Recall that phpMyAdmin created this line of code for us. Good thing too, as it is an easy one to goof up.

```
31. //echo "<p>***********</p>";
32. //echo $query ;
33. //echo "<p>***********</p>";
```

lines 31 - 33 are comments *now*, but previously they were part of the script that printed out the value of the variable **$query**. I had this in there to help me figure out why it didn't work at first, and I leave it in there as an example of what to do when as script doesn't do quite what you thought it would. I then copied the output of line 32 to the clipboard and pasted it into phpMyAdmin for syntax advice.

```
34. if ($mysqli->query($query) === TRUE)
```

line 34 executes a SQL statement "query($query)" then tests for the result of the SQL statement held in the variable $mysqli.

```
35. {
36.  echo "Database table 'INVENTORY' created</P>";
37. }
```

line 36 prints the message "Database table 'INVENTORY' created" if line 34 is a success.

```
38. else
39. {
40.   echo "<p>Error: </p>" . mysql_error();
41. }
```

line 40 prints the message "Error:" and the mySQL error if line 34 fails. Hopefully the value returned by **mysql_error()** will tell you something helpful about why it failed. Sometimes it actually does.

```
42. // Dates are stored in MySQL as 'YYYY-MM-DD' format
```

line 42 is a comment to remind me (and you) to format dates the way mySQL expects them

```
43. $query = "INSERT INTO `cars`.`inventory`
44. (`VIN`, `YEAR`, `Make`, `Model`, `TRIM`, `EXT_COLOR`, `INT_COLOR`, `ASKING_PRICE`, `SALE_PRICE`, `PURCHASE_PRICE`, `MILEAGE`, `TRANSMISSION`, `PURCHASE_DATE`, `SALE_DATE`)
45. VALUES
46. ('5FNYF4H91CB054036', '2012', 'Honda', 'Pilot', 'Touring', 'White Diamond Pearl', 'Leather', '37807', NULL, '34250', '7076', 'Automatic', '2012-11-08', NULL);";
```

lines 43 - 46 changes the value of $query to a new SQL statement, this time an INSERT.

```
49. if ($mysqli->query($query) === TRUE) {
```

line 49 tests for the execution of the SQL statement held in the variable $query

```
50.   echo "<p>Honda Pilot inserted into inventory table. </p>";
```

line 50 prints the message "<p>Honda Pilot inserted into inventory table</p>" if line 49 is a success. The <p> tags put the message on its own line.

```
51. }
52. else
```

```
53. {
54.   echo "<p>Error inserting Honda Pilot: </p>" . mysql_error();
55.   echo "<p>***********</p>";
56.   echo $query ;
57.   echo "<p>***********</p>";
58. }
```

lines 54 - 57 print a message if line 49 fails.

```
60. // Insert a Dodge Durango
61.
62. $query = "INSERT INTO `cars`.`inventory` (`VIN`, `YEAR`, `Make`, `Model`, `TRIM`,
`EXT_COLOR`, `INT_COLOR`, `ASKING_PRICE`, `SALE_PRICE`, `PURCHASE_PRICE`, `MILEAGE`,
`TRANSMISSION`, `PURCHASE_DATE`, `SALE_DATE`)
63. VALUES
64. ('LAKSDFJ234LASKRF2', '2009', 'Dodge', 'Durango', 'SLT', 'Silver', 'Black', '2700', NULL,
'2000', '144000', '4WD Automatic', '2012-12-05', NULL);";
65.
66. If ($mysqli->query($query) === TRUE) {
67.   echo "<p>Dodge Durango inserted into inventory table.</p>";
68. }
69. else
70. {
71.   echo "<p>Error Inserting Dodge: </p>" . mysql_error();
72.   echo "<p>***********</p>";
73.   echo $query ;
74.   echo "<p>***********</p>";
75. }
76.
```

lines 60 -76 does the same thing as 43 - 58, except for a different car.

```
78. $mysqli->close();
```

line 78 closes the connection to mySQL

```
79. ?>
```

line 79 is the end tag for PHP, and any text that followed would be treated as HTML, rather than code.

Hey, where's the HTML?

The astute reader (you!?) might have noticed that this script didn't appear inside the usual pattern of <HTML><Body> <html code here> <php code here> </Body></HTML>.

Yet it worked. How come? I discovered this quite by accident, actually. Most browsers are quite forgiving and will apparently fill in the HTML framework for you if you "forget" to do so, which I did one time. Try it yourself. It works. Is this a best practice? No, I sure isn't!

12

Creating forms to Display, Add, Edit, and Delete data

Introduction

So far we've learned how to use SQL to create databases, add records, edit records, delete records, and select records. Then we learned how to use PHP to perform those same operations.

Next we'll get even more awesome. We'll learn how to use HTML forms along with PHP to create the SQL statements that perform the operation.

Forms that Add Data to a Database

A Basic Form

Let's start with a simple example that is easy to follow. Here's a simple, four-field form:

Sam's Used Cars

VIN: [_____]

Make: [_____]

Model: [_____]

Price: [_____]

[submit]

Obviously, it doesn't have all the attributes of a car that we have previously identified, and it's not very pretty to look at, but it *is* simple, and it will illustrate the point without any extra junk to get in the way of your understanding of the concept.

HTML Code

The code to produce such a form follows

```
<HTML>

<head>
<title>Joy of PHP</title>
</head>

<body>
<h1>Sam's Used Cars
</h1>
<form>
VIN: <input name="VIN" type="text" /><br />
<br />
```

```
Make: <input name="Make" type="text" /><br />
<br />
Model: <input name="Model" type="text" /><br />
<br />
Price: <input name="Asking_Price" type="text" /><br />
<br />
<input name="Submit1" type="submit" value="submit" /><br />
 </form>
</body>

</html>
```

So far what we have is just HTML, and in fact the form won't actually **do anything** if you press the submit button...yet.

Form Action

To make the form actually **do something**, we need to modify the <form> tag. Change the line of code above so that instead of saying **<form>** it says **<form action="SubmitCar.php" method="post">**

This tells the browser that when the form is submitted by pressing the submit button, it should pass this form to the PHP script entitled 'SubmitCar.php' and use the 'Post' method to do so.

> Forms can be submitted either using **method='post'** or **method='get'**. There's really no good reason to use 'get' when submitting a form so to keep things simple, we'll just use 'post' whenever we submit a form.
>
> We'll use post later in the book for a different purpose, though.

PHP Code

Here's what we are going to accomplish. We want the script referenced by the form to get the values from the form, produce a SQL **INSERT** statement using those values, write the SQL statement to the browser so we can see it, execute the SQL statement that we just created, and finally, let us know if it worked.

If all goes well, the script should output something similar to this:

```
INSERT INTO Inventory (VIN, Make, Model, ASKING_PRICE)
VALUES ('9T4BF3EKXBR153775', 'Ford', 'Fiesta', 800)

Connected successfully to mySQL
Selected the Cars database.
You have successfully entered Ford Fiesta into the database.
```

Here's the code for the SubmitCar.php file, which is also available in the sample code. Again, you don't have to study it here because I will walk you through it next. For now, just give it a quick look over.

```
1.<html>
2.<head>
3.  <title>Car Saved</title>
4.</head>
5.<body bgcolor="#FFFFFF" text="#000000" >
6.
7.<?php
8.// Capture the values posted to this php program from the text fields in the form
9.
10.$VIN =  $_POST['VIN'] ;
11.$Make = $_POST['Make'] ;
12.$Model = $_POST['Model'] ;
13.$Price = $_POST['Asking_Price'] ;
14.
15.//Build a SQL Query using the values from above
16.
17.$query = "INSERT INTO Inventory
18. (VIN, Make, Model, ASKING_PRICE)
19.  VALUES (
20.  '$VIN',
21.  '$Make',
22.  '$Model',
```

```
23. $Price
24. )";
25.
26.// Print the query to the browser so you can see it
27.echo ($query. "<br>");
28.
29.$mysqli = new mysqli('localhost', 'root', 'password', 'cars' );
30./* check connection */
31.if (mysqli_connect_errno()) {
32.  printf("Connect failed: %s\n", mysqli_connect_error());
33.  exit();
34.}
35.
36. echo 'Connected successfully to mySQL. <BR>';
37.
38.//select a database to work with
39.$mysqli->select_db("Cars");
40.  Echo ("Selected the Cars database. <br>");
41.
42./* Try to insert the new car into the database */
43.if ($result = $mysqli->query($query)) {
44.  echo "<p>You have successfully entered $Make $Model into the database.</P>";
45.}
46.else
47.{
48.  echo "Error entering $VIN into database: " . mysql_error()."<br>";
49.}
50.$mysqli->close();
51.?>
52.</body>
53.</html>
```

```
1. <html>
```

Line 1 is the opening <html> (which is closed on line 53).

```
2. <head>
3.  <title>Car Saved</title>
```

```
4. </head>
```

Lines 2 – 4 constitute the Head tag, while line 3 sets the page title.

```
5.<body bgcolor="#FFFFFF" text="#000000" >
```

Line 5 opens the body tag (which is closed on line 52). Note that we used the optional parameter to set the background and text colors.

```
7. <?php
```

Line 7 is the opening <php> tag, to signify that the text that follows is code rather than HTML.

```
8. // Capture the values posted to this php program from the text fields in the form
```

Line 8 is a comment. You can never have too many comments in your code. Get in the habit early of over-commenting your code. I have never heard anyone complain that the code they were trying to figure out had "too many" comments distracting from the elegance of the logic.

```
10. $VIN = $_POST['VIN'] ;
11. $Make = $_POST['Make'] ;
12. $Model = $_POST['Model'] ;
13. $Price = $_POST['Asking_Price'] ;
```

Lines 10 – 13 get the values that were on the form and assign them to variables in PHP. $_REQUEST is a special variable that is used to collect data after submitting HTML forms. You follow it with the name of the field on the HTML form that you want to retrieve.

```
15. //Build a SQL Query using the values from above
```

Line 15 is a comment. Comments are good.

```
17.$query = "INSERT INTO Inventory
18. (VIN, Make, Model, ASKING_PRICE)
19.  VALUES (
20.  '$VIN',
```

```
21.  '$Make',
22.  '$Model',
23.  $Price
24.  )";
```

Lines 17 – 24 build a SQL INSERT command. It could have been all on one line, but it is easier to read this way. Notice that the variables $VIN, $Make, $Model, and $Price are put into the formula as they are. Later, when the code is actually executed, PHP will substitute the variable names with their actual values.

```
// Print the query to the browser so you can see it
```

Line 26 is a comment. Comments are good.

```
27.echo ($query. "<br>");
```

Line 27 writes the SQL statement out to the browser, on its own line. The ".
" after the $query adds a <br> to the end of the line. That's what puts it on its own line. Line 27 was not required for the function to work. It is there so you can see how PHP translated the variables into their values when producing the SQL statement, which in turn is stored in the variable $query.

To add two stings together in PHP use the . character. In line 27 we have added two strings together— $query and "<br>", then used the echo command to write it to the browser.

Authors Note: If I was designing PHP, I would use the & character to join two strings. That would make it consistent with other languages, but it is what it is.

```
29. $mysqli = new mysqli('localhost', 'root', 'password', 'cars' );
```

Line 29 makes a connection to the mySQL database by passing the name of the server ('localhost'), username ('root'), password ('password'), and initial database ('cars'). Note your password will likely be different.

```
30. /* check connection */
```

Line 30 is a comment, using the alternate syntax for denoting a comment.

```
31. if (mysqli_connect_errno()) {
32.    printf("Connect failed: %s\n", mysqli_connect_error());
33.    exit();
34. }
```

Lines 31 – 34 test to see if the connection made with line 29 worked or not. If not, it prints an error message then stops further code execution (line 33 – exit). **exit()** is an alternative to the command **die**.

```
36. echo 'Connected successfully to mySQL. <BR>';
```

Line 36 prints to the browser the message 'Connected successfully to mySQL'. This line would not execute if line 33 was called. Since we made it this far, we can conclude that we did in fact connect.

```
38. //select a database to work with
```

Line 38 is a comment that explains the purpose of the next line.

```
39. $mysqli->select_db("Cars");
40.  Echo ("Selected the Cars database. <br>");
```

Line 39 selects the 'cars' database, and **line 40** prints this fact.

```
42./* Try to insert the new car into the database */
```

Line 42 is a comment. You see a theme here, right? The more comments you add, the easier it will be to figure out your code when you come back later to look at it.

```
42. /* Try to insert the new car into the database */
43. if ($result = $mysqli->query($query)) {
```

```
44.  echo "<p>You have successfully entered $Make $Model into the database.</P>";
45. }
46. else
47. {
48.  echo "Error entering $VIN into database: " . mysql_error()."<br>";
49. }
```

Line 43 is the grand finale. Here we actually **execute the SQL statement** against the cars database. **Line 43** is the start of an if statement and **line 44** prints a success message while **line 48** prints a failure message.

```
50. $mysqli->close();
```

Line 50 closes the connection to the mySQL database. This is not strictly required, as the page will still work if you don't do it, but apparently it's a good idea because if you don't do it, eventually the server will develop problems and ultimately require a reboot.

```
51. ?>
```

Line 51 closes the PHP tag that was opened on **line 7**, signaling that the lines that follow are html not PHP code.

```
52.</body>
53.</html>
```

Lines 52 and 53 close the body tag and the HTML tags, respectively.

Wow, we made it through the whole script. If you are still with me, you have a good future in PHP development! Stay with it!

A Brief Time Out...include files

You may recall from the earlier section on *Includes* the notion of reusing code by including the contents of one file in another. This is a good time to revisit this important topic.

So far we've made two different PHP files—the **first** one to create a database and table, and the **second** one in the section above to insert data into the database using a web form. As you can guess from the section headings coming up later in this chapter, we're about to make **even more** scripts that will allow us to edit and delete data as well.

Each of these scripts will have a something in common—code that connects to the mySQL database, and in each case that code will be exactly the same. So far, we've been developing on our own computer, so the host name has been 'LocalHost'. Imagine yourself, sometime in the near future having written a dozen or more scripts into the future, and suddenly you decide to move your application to another computer—one accessible from the Internet. The host name will not be the same. Nor, most likely, will the username and password be the same. What if your password got out and you needed to change it?

Without my helpful intervention **right here**, you would be facing the prospect of changing dozens of .php files—searching for the line that reads something like...

```
$mysqli = new mysqli('localhost', 'root', 'password', 'cars' );
```

...and changing it to reflect the new host name, username, or password. Uck, there would be no joy in that task at all.

From now on, we're going move the part of the code that connects to the database to a separate file, and all our new scripts from this point forward will simply refer to that code using an **include** statement. If any of the values change, we will only have to change it in one place... the file that all the others point to.

Just imagine the joy of changing one line of code and seeing that change propagate across dozens of pages? That's what I'm talking about. The include feature is one of the most useful and **most important** features of PHP, in my humble opinion.

We'll use the line ...

```
include 'db.php';
```

... to tell PHP to insert the contents of the db.php file into the current script.

Forms that Display Summary Data

One of the first things we'll want to do for Sam's Used Cars is to display a list of all the cars that meet the selected criteria. At first, our criteria will be to select **all** the cars, but later on **you** can modify the query to return only certain cars simply by modifying the SELECT statement in the code.

The way this will work is that we will execute a SQL Select statement to retrieve the cars that match the criteria, then loop through all the rows. We'll put each row of data into a nicely formatted table.

Sam's Used Cars

Complete Inventory

Make	Model	Asking Price
Nissan	Maxima	15000.00
Mazda	626	
Mazda	626	1200.00
Toyota	Camry	12000.00
Honda	Pilot	36999.00
Toyota	Camry	18000.00
Toyota	Celica	5000.00
Isusu	Trooper	7700.00

The source code can be found as viewcars.php. If all goes well the page should look like this:

Of course, the output of a simple script is not particularly attractive to look at, but with the addition of a bit of CSS we can make it look like this:

Sam's Used Cars

Complete Inventory

Make	Model	Asking Price
Nissan	Maxima	15000.00
Mazda	626	
Mazda	626	1200.00
Toyota	Camry	12000.00
Honda	Pilot	36999.00
Toyota	Camry	18000.00
Toyota	Celica	5000.00
Isusu	Trooper	7700.00
Ford	Focus	4400.00
Ford	Fiesta	800.00
Mazda	626	
Dodge	Durango	2700.00
Nissan	Rogue	30000.00

But let's not get too far ahead of ourselves. First, here is the code that produces the basic version of the table. The output of this script is more interesting if you have a lot of cars in your database, so if you haven't done so already, use the script "**createdb.php**" included with the sample code to populate your inventory table with a lot of cars.

Code

```
1.<html>
2.<head>
3.  <meta charset="utf-8">
4.  <title>Sam's Used Cars</title>
5.  </head>
6.
7.<body>
8.<h1>Sam's Used Cars</h1>
9.<h3>Complete Inventory</h3>
10. <?php
11.include 'db.php';
12.$query = "SELECT * FROM INVENTORY";
13./* Try to query the database */
14.if ($result = $mysqli->query($query)) {
```

```php
15.  // Don't do anything if successful.
16.}
17.else
18.{
19.  echo "Error getting cars from the database: " . mysql_error()."<br>";
20.}
21.
22.// Create the table headers
23.echo "<table id='Grid' style='width: 80%'><tr>";
24.echo "<th style='width: 50px'>Make</th>";
25.echo "<th style='width: 50px'>Model</th>";
26.echo "<th style='width: 50px'>Asking Price</th>";
27.echo "</tr>\n";
28.
29.$class ="odd"; // Keep track of whether a row was even or odd, so we can style it later
30.
31.// Loop through all the rows returned by the query, creating a table row for each
32.while ($result_ar = mysqli_fetch_assoc($result)) {
33.  echo "<tr class=\"$class\">";
34.  echo "<td>" . $result_ar['Make'] . "</td>";
35.  echo "<td>" . $result_ar['Model'] . "</td>";
36.   echo "<td>" . $result_ar['ASKING_PRICE'] . "</td>";
37.  echo "</td></tr>\n";
38.
39.  // If the last row was even, make the next one odd and vice-versa
40.  if ($class=="odd"){
41.    $class="even";
42.  }
43.  else
44.  {
45.    $class="odd";
46.  }
47.}
48.echo "</table>";
49.$mysqli->close();
50.?>
51.  </body>
52.
53.</html>
```

Code Explained

I won't walk you through **every** line anymore, as I no longer think you need it. From now on, I'll just explain the important ones.

Line 11 is our first use of the **include** option which refers to an external file named db.php which will be included in this script *just as if it were part of the same file.* I highlighted line 11 above in blue, and the code below in blue, in hopes that you would better understand how it works. The content of the blue box below is substituted into the code for the blue line (11) above, so that both files are combined into a single script.

The contents of the 'db.php' file are shown below:

```php
<?php
$mysqli = new mysqli('localhost', 'root', 'mypassword', 'cars' );
/* check connection */
if (mysqli_connect_errno()) {
  printf("Connect failed: %s\n", mysqli_connect_error());
  exit();
}
//select a database to work with
$mysqli->select_db("Cars");

?>
```

The code in the db.php file is identical to the code explained as line 29 in the previous section, so I won't explain it again here. That's another key benefit of include files. Once the code inside it works, you don't really have to think about it much anymore.

```
12.$query = "SELECT * FROM INVENTORY";
```

Line 12 is the query that produces the list of cars to be displayed. In this simple case, we are selecting all the cars.

```
14. if ($result = $mysqli->query($query)) {
15.  // Don't do anything if successful.
16. }
17. else
18. {
19.  echo "Error getting cars from the database: " . mysql_error()."<br>";
20. }
```

Lines 14 – 20 runs the query and displays an error message if the query fails.

```
23. echo "<table id='Grid' style='width: 80%'><tr>";
```

Line 23 is an opening tag to create a table with the ID of 'grid'. The ID is optional but makes it easy to apply styles to the table later. style=width:80% prevents the column from extending to fill the entire screen; instead it takes 80% of the width. <tr> starts the Table Row with the opening <tr> tag.

```
24. echo "<th style='width: 50px'>Make</th>";
25. echo "<th style='width: 50px'>Model</th>";
26. echo "<th style='width: 50px'>Asking Price</th>";
27. echo "</tr>\n";
```

Lines 24– 27 create the first row of the table, the row that contains the column titles of make, model, and price. Line 27 is a closing Table Row tag, followed by a new line.

```
29.  $class ="odd"; // Keep track of whether a row was even or odd, so we can style it later
```

Line 29 sets the value of a variable called $class to 'odd' because the first data row in our table will be odd. As we loop through each row of data, we'll alternately set the $class to the value of either 'odd' or 'even'. We do this so we can style the table later to have alternate rows show different coloring to make it easier on the eyes.

```
31. // Loop through all the rows returned by the query, creating a table row for each
32. while ($result_ar = mysqli_fetch_assoc($result)) {
33.  echo "<tr class=\"$class\">";
34.  echo "<td>" . $result_ar['Make'] . "</td>";
```

```
35. echo "<td>" . $result_ar['Model'] . "</td>";
36. echo "<td>" . $result_ar['ASKING_PRICE'] . "</td>";
37. echo "</td></tr>\n";
```

Lines 31 to 37 create a row in the HTML table to correspond with each row in the database table that we extracted using the query. Each table cell contains data from the mySQL table. For instance, line 34 (echo "<td>" . $result_ar['Make'] . "</td>";) should produce something like:

<td>Ford</td>

because **$result_ar['Make']** says get the value of Make (one of the columns in the table, and in this case 'Ford') and put it here between the <td> tags. Take the time to really understand what that line is doing, because if you can understand this, you can do virtually anything! Remember the . character means join these two strings.

```
39. // If the last row was even, make the next one odd and vice-versa
40. if ($class=="odd"){
41.   $class="even";
42. }
43. else
44. {
45.   $class="odd";
46. }
```

Lines 39 – 46 just alternate the value of $class from even to odd.

```
47. }
```

Line 47 closes the While loop.

```
48. echo "</table>";
```
Line 48 closes the table with the </table> tag.

```
49. $mysqli->close();
```
Line 49 closes the mySQL database

50. ?>

Line 50 indicates the end of the PHP code.

51. </body>

Line 51 is the end of the body in the HTML page.

53. </html>

Finally, **line 53** indicates the end of the HTML

Exercise: Tweaking the SELECT

Go back and modify this code so that it doesn't select **all** the cars but rather a subset that pleases you.

Improving the look of the table with CSS

Here's the CSS that improves the look of the form. This style information is added to the <head> section of the page, but often people put styles into a separate style sheet too. See the file **viewcarswithstyle.php** to see the form in action.

Explaining how CSS works is beyond the scope of this book, and a topic in itself. But the important thing is to see how easily we were able to change the look of the HTML table using a little style information. Take a look at the complete style sheet here, and I'll explain it next.

```
1.<style>
2.  /* The grid is used to format a table */
3.#Grid
4.{
5.font-family:"Trebuchet MS", Arial, Helvetica, sans-serif;
6.width:80%;
7.border-collapse:collapse;
8.margin-left: auto;
9.margin-right: auto;
```

```css
10.}
11.#Grid td, #Grid th
12.{
13.font-size:1em;
14.border:1px solid #61ADD7;
15.padding:3px 7px 2px 7px;
16.}
17.#Grid th
18.{
19.font-size:1.1em;
20.text-align:left;
21.padding-top:5px;
22.padding-bottom:4px;
23.background-color:#C2D9FE;
24.color: lightslategray;
25.
26.}
27.#Grid tr.odd td
28.{
29.color:#000000;
30.background-color: #F2F5A9;
31.}
32.
33.#Grid tr.even
34.{
35.color:#000000;
36.background-color: white;
37.}
38.#Grid head
39.{
40.color:#000000;
41.background-color:teal;
42.}
43.
44. </style>
```

CSS Explained

```
1. <style>
2. /* The grid is used to format a table */
```

Line 1 opens the <style> tag, telling the browser that what follows is a style sheet. Line 2 is a comment.

```
3. #Grid
4. {
5. font-family:"Trebuchet MS", Arial, Helvetica, sans-serif;
6. width:80%;
7. border-collapse:collapse;
8. margin-left: auto;
9. margin-right: auto;
10. }
```

Line 3 says to select an item on the page with the id of Grid. The # symbol is the selector to select something defined using an id, and what follows is the name of the specific thing you want to select. See line 23 of the previous PHP script, which set the id of our table to 'grid' with the line **echo "<table id='Grid' style='width: 80%'>;** Since we have a table with an id='Grid', this style will apply to it.

Everything that follows between the { and the } symbols define the style for that item. We pick font, border, margin, etc.

```
11. #Grid td, #Grid th
12. {
13. font-size:1em;
14. border:1px solid #61ADD7;
15. padding:3px 7px 2px 7px;
16. }
```

Line 11 specifies that the following lines only apply to <td> and <th> tags, if they appear within an item with an ID of 'Grid'.

Each line that follows gets more specific about how an item should be formatted. A specific selector overwrites a general one. So we started off specifying default formatting for Grid, but later we modified specific elements of the grid item. The next bit is how we color alternate rows differently:

```
27.#Grid tr.odd td
28.{
29.color:#000000;
30.background-color: #F2F5A9;
31.}
```

Line 27 says to selects a <td> tag, within a table row <tr> if it is a member of the class odd. Look at the HTML that is output by the script. You'll see a table row for the table defined like this: <tr class='odd'> or <tr class='even'>.

There is another selector for the table headers. It does make sense if you look at it long enough. The # symbol in CSS is a selector. OK, that's it for now. Maybe someday I'll do a "Joy of CSS" book. Let me know...

Modifying the form to link to the detail page

The last thing this form needs is way to link to a specific car. When the site visitor clicks on a specific car in a row, it should take them to more detail about that specific car. In other words, it should take them to the 'car detail' page. We're going to have to make that page, of course.

The <a> tag defines a hyperlink, which is used to link from one page to another. Amazingly, 'A' actually stands for Anchor. I don't associate anchors with jumping around, but I guess someone did, and the tag somehow stuck.

The most important attribute of the <a> element is the href attribute, which indicates the link's destination.

Note that for this to work we will need to **build** the detail page because otherwise the link will naturally fail. Nothing happens automatically. Assuming that the detail page exists, we can modify the code on line 34 that reads as:

```
echo "<td>" . $result_ar['Make'] . "</td>";
```

to instead read as:

```
echo "<td><a href='viewcar.php?VIN=".$result_ar['VIN']."'>" . $result_ar['Make'] .
"</a></td>";
```

What this does is create an 'anchor' or a link which makes the first column of each row a clickable link. It should output HTML similar to:

```
<td><a href='viewcar.php?VIN=123234FE221'>Nissan</a></td>
```

You can see that the URL created will be similar to **/viewcar.php?VIN=123234FE221** as shown above. This tells the browser to open the **viewcar.php** file and pass it the query string of VIN= followed by a VIN. It is called a **query string** because the primary purpose of passing data to a form this way is so it can use the data in a SQL query—and that's exactly what we are going to do.

Remember back when I said to use 'Post' rather then 'Get' when submitting a form? If you *had* used get, clicking the submit button would send to the browser a really long URL with all the field names and values appended to the end of it as a query string in a format similar to *?Make=Ford&Model=Explorer, etc.* We are going to take advantage of that technique to create our own query string and pass it to a script.

For now, clicking on the link will only trigger an error, because the **viewcar.php** file does not yet exist, but that's what we're going to build next.

Forms that Display Detail Data

Once a site visitor has identified a car that they want more information about, the car shopper will want to click on a particular car to learn more about it. So we'll make a PHP page to handle this. We'll call this the Car Detail page, and its file name will be viewcar.php.

Again, we'll keep the example relatively simple for the purpose of following the logic. If all goes well, clicking on a car from the previous screen will bring up a form similar to:

localhost/Joy_of_PHP/viewcar.php?VIN=5FNYF4H91CB054036

Sam's Used Cars

2012 Honda Pilot

Asking Price: 36999.00

Exterior Color: White Diamond Pearl

Interior Color: Leather

Code

```
1.<html >
2.<head>
3.<title>Sam's Used Cars</title>
4.</head>
5.
6.<body>
7.
8.<h1>Sam's Used Cars</h1>
9.<?php include 'db.php';
10.$vin = $_GET['VIN'];
```

```php
11.$query = "SELECT * FROM INVENTORY WHERE VIN='$vin'";
12./* Try to query the database */
13.if ($result = $mysqli->query($query)) {
14.  // Don't do anything if successful.
15.}
16.else
17.{
18.  echo "Sorry, a vehicle with VIN of $vin cannot be found " . mysql_error()."<br>";
19.}
20.// Loop through all the rows returned by the query, creating a table row for each
21.while ($result_ar = mysqli_fetch_assoc($result)) {
22.  $year = $result_ar['YEAR'];
23.    $make = $result_ar['Make'];
24.  $model = $result_ar['Model'];
25.  $trim = $result_ar['TRIM'];
26.  $color = $result_ar['EXT_COLOR'];
27.  $interior = $result_ar['INT_COLOR'];
28.  $mileage = $result_ar['MILEAGE'];
29.  $transmission = $result_ar['TRANSMISSION'];
30.  $price = $result_ar['ASKING_PRICE'];
31.}
32.echo "$year $make $model </p>";
33.echo "<p>Asking Price: $price </p>";
34.echo "<p>Exterior Color: $color </p>";
35.echo "<p>Interior Color: $interior </p>";
36.
37.$mysqli->close();
38.?>
39.
40.</body>
41.</html>
```

Code Explained

```
1. <html >
```

Line 1 opens the HTML tag and starts the document.

```
2.<head>
3.<title>Sam's Used Cars</title>
4.</head>
```

Lines 2 – 4 are the head tags, and in between specifies the document title, 'Sam's Used Cars'.

```
8.<h1>Sam's Used Cars</h1>
```

Line 8 is ordinary HTML; it prints Sam's Used Cars at the top of the page in a headline style type.

```
9. <?php include 'db.php';
```

Line 9 specifies that the current script *include* the db.php file, which logs into the mySQL database.

```
10. $vin = $_GET['VIN'];
```

Line 10 creates a variable called $vin and assigns it the value that follows VIN= in the URL string. Remember, for this form to work, you have to pass it the VIN like this: **/viewcar.php?VIN=123234FE221.** We use the command $_GET because when you submit a form using get the values are appended to the URL in a similar fashion.

```
11. $query = "SELECT * FROM INVENTORY WHERE VIN='$vin'";
```

Line 11 builds a query using the value passed to the form in the Query String, and assigns it to the cleverly named variable $query. See why we call it a 'query string'?

```
12. /* Try to query the database */
```

```
13. if ($result = $mysqli->query($query)) {
14.   // Don't do anything if successful.
15. }
16. else
17. {
18.   echo "Sorry, a vehicle with VIN of $vin cannot be found " . mysql_error()."<br>";
19. }
```

Lines 12 – 19 run the query against the mySQL database and create something called a 'result set'. A result set is the set of data that results from the running of a query. This result set is assigned to the variable $result.

```
20. // Loop through all the rows returned by the query, creating a table row for each
21. while ($result_ar = mysqli_fetch_assoc($result)) {
22.   $year = $result_ar['YEAR'];
23.   $make = $result_ar['Make'];
24.   $model = $result_ar['Model'];
25.   $trim = $result_ar['TRIM'];
26.   $color = $result_ar['EXT_COLOR'];
27.   $interior = $result_ar['INT_COLOR'];
28.   $mileage = $result_ar['MILEAGE'];
29.   $transmission = $result_ar['TRANSMISSION'];
30.   $price = $result_ar['ASKING_PRICE'];
31. }
```

Lines 20 – 31 loop through 'all' the rows returned as a result of the query. In our case, since VINs are unique we would only expect to get one row of data back, but we are using basically the same technique we learned in the prior section – Forms that Display Summary Data.

```
22.   $year = $result_ar['YEAR'];
23.   $make = $result_ar['Make'];
...
```

Lines 22 to 30 assign a series of variables with the values of the specified data columns, which match the names of the columns in the database table 'inventory'.

```
31. }
```

Line 31 closes the while loop.

Forms that Edit Data

If you understand how to make *Forms that Add Data to a Database,* and you understand *Forms that Display Detail Data,* it isn't much of a stretch (conceptually anyway) to make a form that Edits data. Simply create a form just like the one you made to add data, but before displaying it retrieve data from the database and pre-populate it with values.

Instead of executing a SQL Insert command when the user clicks submit, instead execute an Update.

Forms that Delete Data

To delete a specific record from a database, you need a way for the user to select the data they want to delete. You already learned how to do this in the section *Forms that Display Summary Data.* In the section *Modifying the form to link to the detail page* we created an <HREF> link that takes the user to a detail page, and you can use that same technique to take them to a delete page, such as the one shown below:

Code to delete data

```
1.<html>
2.<head>
3.<title>Sam's Used Cars</title>
4.</head>
5.<body>
6.<h1>Sam's Used Cars</h1>
7.<?php
8.include 'db.php';
9.$vin = $_GET['VIN'];
10.$query = "DELETE FROM INVENTORY WHERE VIN='$vin'";
11.echo "$query <BR>";
```

```
12./* Try to execute the DELETE against the database
13.
14.if ($result = $mysqli->query($query)) {
15.  Echo "The vehicle with VIN $vin has been deleted.";
16.}
17.else
18.{
19.  echo "Sorry, a vehicle with VIN of $vin cannot be found " . mysql_error()."<br>";
20.}
21.
22.$mysqli->close();
23.
24.?>
25.
26.</body>
27.</html>
```

Code Explained

```
1.<html>
2.<head>
3.<title>Sam's Used Cars</title>
4.</head>
5.<body>
6.<h1>Sam's Used Cars</h1>
```

Lines 1 – 6 set up the basics of the page. We open an <html>, open and close the <head> tags, and start the body with a headline proclaiming "Sam's Used Cars".

```
7. <?php
8. include 'db.php';
```

Lines 6 – 7 are also familiar to us by now. We open the php tag and add the insert line to connect us to our mySQL database.

```
9.  $vin = $_GET['VIN'];
10. $query = "DELETE FROM INVENTORY WHERE VIN='$vin'";
11. echo "$query <BR>";
```

Line 9 gets the VIN from the query string. Remember, this page will be called with ?VIN='23ABC..' appended to the end. **Line 10** builds a SQL delete statement using the VIN, so we know which vehicle to delete. **Line 11** simply writes the query to screen so we can see the query we built. It is not strictly required for the function to work.

```
14. if ($result = $mysqli->query($query)) {
15.  Echo "The vehicle with VIN $vin has been deleted.";
16. }
17. else
18. {
19.  echo "Sorry, a vehicle with VIN of $vin cannot be found " . mysql_error()."<br>";
20. }
```

Lines 14 through 20 do the actual work. Line 14 performs the query, and returns True if the query succeeds. If so, line 15 prints a success message to the screen, and if not, line 19 prints a failure message to the screen.

```
22. $mysqli->close();
23.
24. ?>
25.
26. </body>
27. </html>
```

The rest of the page close the database connection, closes the php tag, closes the body tag, and finally closes the html tag.

Exercise

To add edit and delete functionality, simply add two new columns to the table with the links for edit and delete, and call the appropriate php page. **deletecar.php** has been provided, while **editcar.php** you will have to make yourself. If you *absolutely can't* get **editcar.php** to work, I did include it in the sample code. Just do yourself a favor and TRY to make it.

For the answer to this challenge, look at the sample page **viewcarswithstyle2.php**, which is included in the sample code.

13

Session Variables

Introduction

Variables in PHP typically have a specific and limited scope—generally, a variable is only available on the page on which it was declared. The prime exception to this rule is when you declare a variable inside a function, it only works in that function.

But what if you want access to the **same** variable across multiple pages in your application? For instance, I'm a regular shopper on Amazon.com. If you are too, you may have noticed that once you're logged in, **every page** has your name on the top of it.

Presumably, there is a variable in a script somewhere called something like $FirstName containing the value 'Alan'. By now, you could probably easily write such a script. Here's a hint:

```
echo "$FirstName's Amazon.com";
```

But how does that value $FirstName pass from page to page as I wander about the site? And how does the site keep track of hundreds of unique $FirstName variables for all the unique customers who happen to be on the site at the same time? The answer is session variables.

Sessions

A session variable is a special kind of variable that, once set, is available to all the pages in an application for as long as the user has their browser open, or until the session is explicitly terminated by the developer (you).

The great thing about session variables is that PHP will magically keep track of which particular session variable goes with each particular user. So while my Amazon.com experience will always say *"Alan's Amazon"*, yours will say something different (unless your name also happens to be Alan, of course.) Sessions work by creating a unique id (UID) for each visitor and storing variables based on this UID. The UID is typically stored in a cookie.

A cookie, also known as an HTTP cookie, web cookie, or browser cookie, is a small piece of data sent from a website and stored in a user's web browser while a user is browsing a website.

It doesn't really matter *how* they work, the important thing is that they *do* work. And, they are very cool. They open up a whole realm of possibilities for customizing your web application for a specific customer. For example, in the case of **Sam's Used Cars**, you could ask a customer their preferred car color, make/model, features, etc. From that point on, you can customize the pages to reflect the customers' preferences. For example, *Hey look, this car has a sunroof!* (And it's red too!) It's just a sample app, so it's OK to code annoying features to learn something valuable.

Once a user closes their browser, the cookie will be erased and the session will end. So sessions are not a good place to store data you intend to keep for long. The right place to store long-term data is in a database. Of course, sessions and databases *can* work together. For instance, you can store a user's preferences in a database, and retrieve them from the database when the user "logs in" or types in their email address or does whatever it is that you coded for them to identify themselves. Once the data is retrieved, assign the preferences to the session variables and they will be available from then on.

Starting a PHP Session

Before you can store user information in your PHP session, you must first start up the session using the **session_start()** function. The session_start() function **must** appear BEFORE the <html> tag, or it won't work.

```
<?php session_start(); ?>

<html>
<body>
<p>Hello world</p>
</body>
</html>
```

The code above will start the user's session with the server and allow you to start saving user information into session variables.

Using Session Variables

The correct way to store and retrieve session variables is to use the PHP **$_SESSION** variable:

Store a variable

```
<?php
session_start();
// store session data
$_SESSION['FirstName']='Alan';
?>

<html>
<body>
```

Retrieve a variable

```php
<?php
//retrieve session data
echo $_SESSION['FirstName']."'s Amazon";
?>
```

Output: **Alan's Amazon**

Checking for a variable

You can check to see if a session variable is available or not by using the **isset()** function.

> bool **isset** (mixed $var [, mixed $...])
>
> Determines if a variable is set and is not NULL. You can unset a variable with **unset()**.

Here's an example:

```php
<?php
session_start();
if(isset($_SESSION['FirstName']))
echo $_SESSION['FirstName']."'s Amazon";
else
$_SESSION['views']-1;
echo "Welcome to Amazon";
?>
```

Destroying a Session

If you wish to delete some session data, you can use the **unset()** function. If you want to delete it all, use the **session_destroy()** function. The **unset()** function is used to delete a specific session variable:

```php
<?php
session_start();
```

```
if(isset($_SESSION['FirstName']))
  unset($_SESSION['FirstName']);
?>
```

You can also completely destroy all the session by calling the
session_destroy() function:

```
<?php
  session_destroy();
?>
```

Note: session_destroy() will reset your session and you will lose all your stored session data. This is an easy way to implement a logout function.

14

Working with Images

Introduction

A used car web site would not be of much use to the typical car shopper without providing images of the cars, so in this chapter we will cover how to add images to our site. It would be rather simple if each car had a single image associated with it— in that case we could simply add an additional column to our inventory table called 'image' (or something equally descriptive, such as 'primary_image') which would store the file name of the image associated with the particular car.

Then we would build PHP to retrieve the image name and insert it into an HTML image tag on the car details page.

To display an image in your HTML page, use the syntax **<img src="filename">** in the simplest form or add optional parameters to specify height and width, and text to display if the image isn't available (or for screen readers) such as **<img src="smiley.gif" alt="Smiley face" height="42" width="42">**

Of course, PHP would be well suited for this. We would read the file name from the database and use PHP to create the image tag dynamically.

For instance, we *could* modify our earlier example which shows the detail for a specific car by adding the lines highlighted in red as follows:

```
1.<html >
2.<head>
3.<title>Sam's Used Cars</title>
4.</head>
5.
6.<body>
7.
8.<h1>Sam's Used Cars</h1>
9.<?php include 'db.php';
10.$vin = $_GET['VIN'];
11.$query = "SELECT * FROM INVENTORY WHERE VIN='$vin'";
12./* Try to query the database */
13.if ($result = $mysqli->query($query)) {
14.  // Don't do anything if successful.
15.}
16.else
17.{
18.  echo "Sorry, a vehicle with VIN of $vin cannot be found " . mysql_error()."<br>";
19.}
20.// Loop through all the rows returned by the query, creating a table row for each
21.while ($result_ar = mysqli_fetch_assoc($result)) {
22.  $year = $result_ar['YEAR'];
23.    $make = $result_ar['Make'];
24.  $model = $result_ar['Model'];
25.  $trim = $result_ar['TRIM'];
26.  $color = $result_ar['EXT_COLOR'];
27.  $interior = $result_ar['INT_COLOR'];
28.  $mileage = $result_ar['MILEAGE'];
29.  $transmission = $result_ar['TRANSMISSION'];
30.  $price = $result_ar['ASKING_PRICE'];
31.    $image =$result_ar['Primary_Image'];
32.}
33.echo "$year $make $model </p>";
34.echo "<p>Asking Price: $price </p>";
```

```
35.echo "<p>Exterior Color: $color </p>";
36.echo "<p>Interior Color: $interior </p>";
37.echo "<IMG src='$image'>";
38.
39.$mysqli->close();
40.?>
41.
42.</body>
43.</html>
```

This example assumes that we have a column in our database called **Primary_Image**, which contains the file name of an image file that is stored on our server. The sample files home page contains a script that makes this modification, if you are so inclined.

If the images were in a folder called 'images', the line would read:

```
echo "<IMG src='images\$image'>";
```

Exercise: Viewing Images

Get the above example to work. Create an images folder underneath the folder that is running the car lot application and put some images into it. Modify your inventory table to add a **Primary_Image** field and enter some values in that field to associate specific cars with specific images.

Make a copy of the **viewcar.php** script (call it viewcar-backup.php in case you need it later), then modify the **viewcar.php** as shown in red above so that it reads the image location out of the database and inserts the image into the page using the <img> tag.

Pulling an unknown number of images from a database

Assuming you got the above exercise to work, you must admit that it is pretty slick. Congratulations, you are officially awesome. But, we can do **much more**. Just having *one* image of a car doesn't really reflect the reality of a visitor's expectation of a car site. More likely a visitor to Sam's Used Cars web site would want to see *many* images of a car he or she is interested in, and our site will have to accommodate this. Some cars might have only one image, but some might have 10 or more. It will be different for each car. So how would we accomplish this? Having a single column called **Primary_Image** is obviously not the permanent solution. As soon as you show it to Sam, he'll surely say 'But what if I have two pictures of the car to show?' That's the nature of web development sometimes. One good idea sparks another. Don't get frustrated when this happens, but rather think to yourself, *'Wow, I inspired an even better idea!'*

The easiest way to handle a variable number of images would be to create a database table to store them in.

Let's add a table called 'images' to our cars database. It should have the columns ID, VIN, and ImageFile.

Exercise: Create a Database Table to store images

Use phpMyAdmin to create this table, like so.

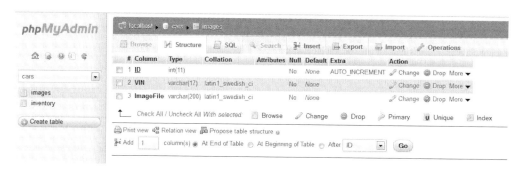

Now you need to populate the table with some sample data. Here's what I did. Go to http://www.cars.com and search for some cars. Copy the VIN to the clipboard, and save some the pictures of the car to your hard drive. Enter a row in the images table for each of the images you save, and enter the VIN of the car for each one. There should also be a corresponding entry in the inventory table for that car, with the exact same VIN. It's easy to do in phpMyAdmin. Don't worry about trying to automate that part of it yet.

Exercise: Modify the viewcar.php page to show multiple images

Once you have some sample data that matches up specific VINs with specific images, it's actually pretty easy to display those images on the page along with the description of the car. Here's a code snippet you can append to the **viewcars.php** form to extract the names of the images for the selected car.

The assumption of this script is you have the VIN of the car in the variable $vin, and that you have included 'db.php' to establish the database connection.

```
1.<?php
2.$query = "SELECT * FROM images WHERE VIN='$vin'";
3./* Try to query the database */
4.if ($result = $mysqli->query($query)) {
5.  // Got some results
6.  // Loop through all the rows returned by the query, creating a table row for each
7.while ($result_ar = mysqli_fetch_assoc($result)) {
8.  $image = $result_ar['ImageFile'];
9.  echo "<img src='uploads/$image' width= '250'> " ;
10.}
11.}
12.$mysqli->close();
```

Code explained

```
2. $query = "SELECT * FROM images WHERE VIN='$vin'";
```

Line 2 sets up the query whereby we select all the fields in the images table for the specific car (WHERE VIN=).

```
4. if ($result = $mysqli->query($query)) {
```

Line 4 runs the query and checks to see if any results were returned from the database.

```
7. while ($result_ar = mysqli_fetch_assoc($result)) {
8.   $image = $result_ar['ImageFile'];
9.   echo "<img src='uploads/$image' width= '250'> ";
10. }
```

Lines 7 – 10 loops through the result set as many times as there are rows. In other words, if there were five images for a specific car, there would be five rows of data returned and the while loop would go around five times.

```
11. }
12. $mysqli->close();
```

Line 11 closes the if statement and the line 12 closes the connection to the mySQL database.

15

PHP File Uploads

Introduction

In the previous section, we captured images for our cars and then saved them manually onto the hard drive. That's cool, but tedious. What would be *really* cool would be to simply select a car in our inventory and click a button called "Add Image", and let the script handle the rest – putting the file in the right place and creating the correct row in the images table using the VIN of the selected vehicle.

That's what we'll do next.

Create an Upload File form

In its most basic incarnation, here is an HTML form you can use to upload a file.

```
<html>
<body>

<form action="upload_file.php" method="post" enctype="multipart/form-data">
<label for="file">Filename:</label>
<input type="file" name="file" id="file"><br>
```

```
<input type="submit" name="submit" value="Submit">
</form>

</body>
</html>
```

There are a couple of things worth pointing out.

First, notice the form attributes: action='upload_file.php' means that when you click the submit button, the result of the form post will be passed to the **upload_file.php** script for further processing. Next, the enctype="multipart/form-data" is a new one for us. Here we are specifying the encoding type to be used by the form. You have to specify that it is **multipart/form-data** if you are including a file upload control on a form, so the browser knows to pass the file as a file, and not as just another big block of text.

We also have a new type of input box. In the past, we've been using the input boxes mostly to allow users to type in text. When you specify that an input type="file" the browser handles it differently. It will put a browse button next to the input field, allowing the user to select a file from his or her computer.

Create a Script to Process the Uploaded File

The form above specified that the post be processed by 'upload_file.php'. This script is used to do something with the file once its been uploaded. The script that follows simply echoes back to the browser *some* of the attributes of the file that has just been uploaded. There are, of course, other file attributes that we won't cover, because you probably won't ever need to use them. Just know that they are there.

```php
<?php
if ($_FILES["file"]["error"] > 0)
  {
  echo "Error: " . $_FILES["file"]["error"] . "<br>";
```

```
}
else
{
echo "Upload: " . $_FILES["file"]["name"] . "<br>";
echo "Type: " . $_FILES["file"]["type"] . "<br>";
echo "Size: " . ($_FILES["file"]["size"] / 1024) . " kB<br>";
echo "Stored in: " . $_FILES["file"]["tmp_name"];
}
?>
```

I highlighted in yellow the parts that need to match. In other words, if the name of the input control on the upload form refers to the file as 'foo', like <input type="file" name="foo"> you would **also** have refer to it as foo on the script that follows, such as $_FILES["foo"]["name"]. The actual name doesn't matter, but what does matter is consistency.

When you upload a file using PHP, the file is stored in a temporary folder. Unless you specifically do *something* with the file, it will soon disappear.

For Sam's Used Cars, the ideal thing to do would be to upload the file, copy the file into a specific folder, and then create a record in the images table that inserts the proper vehicle VIN and the file name of the image we just uploaded. In the sample data, see the script ViewCarsAddImage.php to see this exact concept in action.

Code: ViewCarsAddImage.php

```
1.<?php
2. include 'db.php';
3. $vin = trim($_POST['VIN']);
4.if ($_FILES["file"]["error"] > 0)
5. {
6. echo "Error: " . $_FILES["file"]["error"] . "<br>";
7. }
8.else
9. {
```

```
10. echo "Upload: " . $_FILES["file"]["name"] . "<br>". "\n";
11. echo "Type: " . $_FILES["file"]["type"] . "<br>". "\n";
12. echo "Size: " . ($_FILES["file"]["size"] / 1024) . " kB<br>". "\n";
13. echo "VIN: ".$vin."<br>";
14. echo "Stored temporarily as: " . $_FILES["file"]["tmp_name"]."<br><BR>". "\n";
15. $currentfolder = getcwd();
16. echo "This script is running in: ".$currentfolder."<br>". "\n";
17. $target_path = getcwd() ."/uploads/";
18. echo "The uploaded file will be stored in the folder: ".$target_path."<br>". "\n";
19.
20. $target_path = $target_path . basename( $_FILES['file']['name']);
21. $imagename = "uploads/". basename( $_FILES['file']['name']);
22. echo "The full file name of the uploaded file is '". $target_path."'<br>". "\n";
23.
24. echo "The relative name of the file for use in the IMG tag is " . $imagename ."<br><br>". "\n";;
25.
26.if(move_uploaded_file($_FILES['file']['tmp_name'], $target_path)) {
27.  echo "The file ". basename( $_FILES['file']['name']). " has been uploaded<br>". "\n";
28.
29.  // Create a database entry for this image
30.  if (mysqli_connect_errno()) {
31.    printf("Connect failed: %s\n", mysqli_connect_error());
32.    exit();
33.  }
34.
35. echo 'Connected successfully to mySQL. <BR>';
36. $file_name = $_FILES["file"]["name"];
37. $query = "INSERT INTO images (VIN, ImageFile) VALUES ('$vin', '$file_name')";
38. echo $query."<br>\n";
39.  echo "<a href='AddImage.php?VIN=";
40.  echo $vin;
41.  echo "'>Add another image for this car </a></p>\n";
42./* Try to insert the new car into the database */
43.if ($result = $mysqli->query($query)) {
44.    echo "<p>You have successfully entered $target_path into the database.</P>\n";
45.
46.  }
47.  else
```

```
48. {
49.   echo "Error entering $VIN into database: " . mysql_error()."<br>";
50. }
51. $mysqli->close();
52. echo "<img src='$imagename' width='150'><br>";
53.
54.} else{
55.   echo "There was an error uploading the file, please try again!";
56.}
57. }
58.
59. include 'footer.php'
60.?>
```

Code Explained

```
1.<?php
2. include 'db.php';
```

Line 1 opens the PHP tag. and **line 2** adds the necessary include file to connect to our database.

```
3. $vin = trim($_POST['VIN']);
```

Line 3 creates a variable called $vin and assigns it the value that was passed to it using when a form was posted. Again, see this in action with the sample scripts included with this book. This is not the only way we could have done this. We could also have passed the VIN in a query string, the technique we used in **viewcar.php**

```
4. if ($_FILES["file"]["error"] > 0)
5. {
6.   echo "Error: " . $_FILES["file"]["error"] . "<br>";
7. }
```

Lines 4 – 7 test to see if a file was, in fact, uploaded. If not, an error is printed using line 6.

```
8. else
9. {
```

Beginning with **Line 9**, the script begins to process the uploaded file.

```
10. echo "Upload: " . $_FILES["file"]["name"] . "<br>". "\n";
11. echo "Type: " . $_FILES["file"]["type"] . "<br>". "\n";
12. echo "Size: " . ($_FILES["file"]["size"] / 1024) . " kB<br>". "\n";
13. echo "VIN: ".$vin."<br>";
```

Lines 10 – 12 print information about the file, and **line 13** prints the VIN, just to make sure we got it without any problems.

```
14. echo "Stored temporarily as: " . $_FILES["file"]["tmp_name"]."<br><BR>". "\n";
```

Line 14 tells us the name that PHP used to temporarily store the uploaded file.

TIP: Notice that on the end of the line I also have it write "\n", which means to add a new line at the end of this. This doesn't affect the script at all, but it does put a new line on the HTML that is created by the script. Putting \n at the end of the line on scripts makes the HTML code easier to read when you look at a page and select View Source— something that every PHP developer has to do from time to time.

```
15. $currentfolder = getcwd();
16. echo "This script is running in: " .$currentfolder."<br>". "\n";
```

Line 15 uses the command **getcwd()** to figure out the name of the folder in which the current script is running. Why did I want that? Because I want to put the uploaded file into a folder that is under the current folder, and to do *that* you need to know where you are. **Line 16** outputs what it just learned.

> **getcwd()** The getcwd() function returns the current directory. This function returns the current directory on success and FALSE on failure.

```
17. $target_path = getcwd() ."/uploads/";
```

In **line 17**, we create a variable called $target_path and assign it a value by adding two strings together using the . character. The two strings we added are the current directory and /uploads/. We are creating the target path to specify where we want the uploaded file to be put— in the uploads folder.

```
18. echo "The uploaded file will be stored in the folder: ".$target_path."<br>". "\n";
```

Line 18 outputs the result of the calculation to set the target path.

```
20. $target_path = $target_path . basename( $_FILES['file']['name']);
```

In **line 20** we tweak the target path yet again, this time appending the original file name of the uploaded file to it.

```
21. $imagename = "uploads/". basename( $_FILES['file']['name']);
```

Line 21 calculates the name of just the image file without the entire file path. This is because when you are working with HTML <img> tags, you don't have to specify the entire path of the image; you only need to specify where it is *relative to where you are.*

```
22. echo "The full file name of the uploaded file is '". $target_path."'<br>". "\n";
23.
24. echo "The relative name of the file for use in the IMG tag is " . $imagename ."<br><br>". "\n";
```

Lines 22 and 24 output the values of these calculations so you can see what was the result. Of course, if this was a "real" web site for a used car lot, you wouldn't want all this extra information going to the browser.

> The reason for all these echo statements is so you can follow along with the code as it executes.

```
26. if(move_uploaded_file($_FILES['file']['tmp_name'], $target_path)) {
27.   echo "The file ". basename( $_FILES['file']['name']). " has been uploaded<br>". "\n";
```

Lines 26 moves the uploaded file from the temporary location assigned by PHP into the target path that you calculated in line 20. **Line 27** informs you of this fact.

```
29. // Create a database entry for this image
30. if (mysqli_connect_errno()) {
31.   printf("Connect failed: %s\n", mysqli_connect_error());
32.   exit();
33. }
34.
35. echo 'Connected successfully to mySQL. <BR>';
```

Next, we want to create a record in the images table that points to this new image file. **Lines 29 to 35** set the stage for this to happen.

```
36. $file_name = $_FILES["file"]["name"];
37. $query = "INSERT INTO images (VIN, ImageFile) VALUES ('$vin', '$file_name')";
38. echo $query."<br>\n";
```

In **line 36** we get just the name of the uploaded file, without any path information at all. This is because we just want to insert the name of the file into the database. When referring to the file later with an <IMG> tag, we can always specify a path if needed.

Line 37 builds the query to insert the record into the database, and line 38 writes out what the query is. Line 38 was very helpful while I was originally writing this script, because of course it didn't work the first time I tried it. Seeing the actual query is the first step to figuring out why a particular query did not work.

```
39. echo "<a href='AddImage.php?VIN=";
40. echo $vin;
41. echo "'>Add another image for this car </a></p>\n";
```

Lines 39 to 41 create a link that allows us to easily add another image for this car if we have one.

```
42. /* Try to insert the new car into the database */
43. if ($result = $mysqli->query($query)) {
44.    echo "<p>You have successfully entered $target_path into the database.</P>\n";
45.
46. }
47. else
48. {
49.    echo "Error entering $VIN into database: " . mysql_error()."<br>";
50. }
51. $mysqli->close();
```

Lines 42 to 51 execute the query and prints out either a success or failure message. Line 52 closes the connection to mySQL.

```
52.  echo "<img src='$imagename' width='150'><br>";
```

Line 52 creates an image tag for the file we just uploaded so you can see what it looks like. When I first created this the images were so big they took over the whole screen, so I added the attribute width='150' to keep the images to a reasonable size. This tells the browser to resize the image.

16

PHP Quirks and Tips

Introduction

Every language has its quirks. As I encounter those aspects of PHP that are not immediately intuitive, or if I find a great tip that could make your life easier, it will go into this section.

Single Quotes vs Double Quotes

When working with strings, it is important to understand the difference in how PHP treats single quotes (echo 'Hello $name';) as compared with double quotes (echo "Hello $name";)

Single quoted strings will display things exactly "as is." Variables will not be substituted for their values. The first example above (echo 'Hello $name';) will print out Hello $name.

Double quote strings will display a host of escaped characters and variables in the strings will be substituted for their values. The second example above (echo "Hello $name") will print out Hello Alan if the $name variable contains 'Alan'.

This is an easy thing to mix up, so read it again. :)

The Equal Sign

The equal sign can often be a source of confusion. A single equal sign is used to **assign** a value to a variable, for instance $FirstName = 'Alan';

The equal sign can also be used to **compare** to values, if you put two of them together and include it in an **if** statement. For instance, $FirstName == 'Alan' will return true for me, as the following code demonstrates

```php
<?php
$FirstName = 'Alan';
if ($FirstName == "Alan")
{
echo "Hello Mr. Awesome";
}
else
{
echo "Hello $FirstName";
}
?>
```

See the sample code comparisons.php

The quirky thing about the double equal test is that PHP will attempt to convert the two variables being compared into different types to see if it gets a match. For instance, if $a = 1 and $b = "1" you might think that they are not equal because they are different types. (One is a *number* and the other is a *string*.)

However, comparing $a and $b using the == comparison will return **true**, because if you convert $b from the type string to the type number the two variables are equal.

When you convert a variable from one type to another type, that's called

'Casting'. I could also have written that PHP will cast the string into a number, then find the two variables equal, but you have to admit that does sound awful geeky. But I mention it because you may well come across the term.

If you want to test if two values are the same value **and** the same type, you compare them using **three** equal signs. This way, $a === $b would return false.

```
<html>
<body>
<h1>Comparison Operators</h1>
<?php
$FirstName = 'Alan';
if ($FirstName == "Alan")
{
echo "Hello Master";
}
else
{
echo "Hello $FirstName";
}
echo "<br>";
$a = 1;
$b = "1";
if ($a == $b)
{
echo '$a is equal to $b';
}
else
{
echo '$a is not equal to $b';
}

echo "<br><BR>";
if ($a === $b)
{
echo '$a is equal to $b';
}
else
{
echo '$a is not equal to $b';
}
```

```
?>
</body>
</html>
```

Comparison Operators

Example	Name	Result
$a == $b	Equal	TRUE if $a is equal to $b after type juggling.
$a === $b	Identical	TRUE if $a is equal to $b, and they are of the same type.
$a != $b	Not equal	TRUE if $a is not equal to $b after type juggling.
$a <> $b	Not equal	TRUE if $a is not equal to $b after type juggling.
$a !== $b	Not identical	TRUE if $a is not equal to $b, or they are not of the same type.
$a < $b	Less than	TRUE if $a is strictly less than $b.
$a > $b	Greater than	TRUE if $a is strictly greater than $b.
$a <= $b	Less than or equal to	TRUE if $a is less than or equal to $b.
$a >= $b	Greater than or equal to	TRUE if $a is greater than or equal to $b.

If you compare a number with a string or if the comparison involves numerical strings, then each string is converted to a number and the comparison performed numerically. These rules also apply to the switch statement. The type conversion does not take place when the comparison is === or !== as this involves comparing the type as well as the value.

17

Security Considerations

Introduction

As we have seen, PHP is a very easy language to learn, and many people without any sort of formal background in programming will learn it as a way to add interactivity to their web sites.

Unfortunately, that often means PHP programmers, especially those newer to web development, are unaware of the potential security risks their web applications can contain.

Security is something that is often overlooked when designing a web project, because there isn't really any "joy" in thinking about someone hacking into your shiny new application.

Security is a difficult thing to measure, and it is impossible to say whether an application is completely secure or not-- there are only *degrees* of security. Naturally, the more effort you put into making an application secure, the more secure it will be. The trick, of course, is finding the right balance in time and effort— and expense.

Suffice it to say that the examples used in this book were not designed with security in mind, they were designed with ease of learning in mind.

It is fairly easy and relatively inexpensive to provide a "sufficient" level of security for most applications. However, if your security needs are very demanding— because the information stored in your application is very valuable (or very sensitive, like nuclear launch codes) then you must ensure a higher level of security despite the increased costs that will be associated with it. Remember, a security breach can also be very expensive.

Balancing Security and Usability

Sadly, many of the steps taken to increase the security of a web application also decrease its usability. Passwords, session time-outs, and access control levels and roles all create obstacles for legitimate users. While these steps will increase the security of the application, you can't have it so secure that nobody can use it.

I did a year-plus contract as a developer at an unnamed government agency that claimed to be very security conscious. They required a thorough background check prior to employment, and everyone had to wear high-tech badges to move about the building. We even had guards at the entrance to the building. It was "so secure" that we had to change our passwords every 30 days to a password we hadn't used before, and that password had to be at least 10 characters long and contain numbers, letters, mixed case, and punctuation marks— and it couldn't be found in the dictionary.

In short, they required passwords that no human could actually remember, and the system was not very usable. If your computer was idle for 15 minutes or more you'd be prompted to type in the password in again. **Everyone** I worked with on that project had their password *written down on a piece of paper **right next to** their computer*. Clearly the "powers that be" in the security department had picked security over usability to such an extreme that the very security they were seeking was utterly compromised.

SQL Injection

One of PHP's greatest strengths is the ease with which it can communicate with databases, such as MySQL. The **Sam's Used Car Lot** example from this book and thousands of other high profile web sites, such as http://Facebook.com, rely on databases to function.

With that strength also comes risks. The most common security hazard faced when interacting with a database is something called SQL Injection - when a user deliberately uses part of your application to run unauthorized and unintended SQL queries on your database.

Let's use a common example. Although we didn't cover it in this book, many systems that ask a user to login feature a line of PHP code that looks a lot like this one:

```
$authorized = mysql_query("SELECT Username, Password, UserLevel FROM Users WHERE
Username = '".$_POST['username']."' and Password = '".$_POST['password']."'");
```

The script takes the username and password that was entered on the form and builds a query using the text entered by the user.

Does it look familiar? You'll see many variations of this as your journey into the Joy of PHP continues. So what's the problem? It does not look like such code could do much damage. But let's say for a moment that I enter the following into the "username" input box in the form and submit it:

```
' OR 1=1 #
```

The hash symbol (#) tells MySQL that everything following it is a comment and to ignore it. The query that is going to be executed by mySQL will now look like this:

```
SELECT Username, Password FROM Users
     WHERE Username = '' OR 1=1 #' and Password = ''
```

The # symbol tells mySQL to ignore any text that follows, leaving a WHERE statement of 'WHERE Username = '' OR 1=1'. Since 1 **always** equals 1, the WHERE clause of the SQL will match for **every** row—and here's the bad part. The query will return **all** of the usernames and passwords from the database. What may happen next is that if the first username and password combination is the admin user, then the person who simply entered a few symbols into a username box is now logged in as your website administrator, *as if* they actually knew the admin's username and password, which they probably don't, and shouldn't know.

With a little creativity which is beyond the scope of this book, SQL Injection can be used to accomplish some nasty tricks you probably never thought of when designing your application.

Fortunately, it is pretty easy to put up road-blocks that help prevent this type of vulnerability. By checking for apostrophes in the items we enter into the database, and removing or substituting them, we can prevent anyone from running their own SQL code on our database.

The function below would do the trick:

```
function make_safe($variable) {
  $variable = mysql_real_escape_string(trim($variable));
  return $variable;
}
```

Next we would need to modify our query. Instead of directly using the **_POST** variables, we would pass all user-provided data through the make_safe function, such as:

```
$username = make_safe($_POST['username']);
$password = make_safe($_POST['password']);
```

```
$authorized = mysql_query("SELECT Username, Password, UserLevel FROM Users WHERE
Username = '".$username."' and Password = '".$password."'");
```

Now, if a user entered the malicious data above, the query will look like the following, which is perfectly harmless. The following query will select from a database where the username is equal to "\' OR 1=1 #".

```
SELECT Username, Password, UserLevel FROM Users
     WHERE Username = '\' OR 1=1 #' and Password = ''
```

Now, unless you happen to have a user with a very unusual username and a blank password, your attacker will not be able to do any damage.

It is important to check **all** the data passed to your database like this, however secure you may think it is.

Additional Resources

See also http://www.addedbytes.com/articles/writing-secure-php/writing-secure-php-1/

http://phpsec.org/projects/guide/

18

Appendix A: Installing PHP on a Website

How to install on a Windows Server

Microsoft has conveniently automated the entire process for Microsoft servers. All you need to do is visit http://www.microsoft.com/web/gallery/install.aspx?appid=PHP53.

Supported Operating Systems are Windows 8, Windows 7, Windows Vista SP2, Windows XP SP3+, Windows Server 2003 SP2+, Windows Server 2008, Windows Server 2008 R2, and Windows Server 2012.

You must have administrator privileges on your computer to run the Web Platform Installer.

Here's a document describing how to install PHP on Windows Server 2008 http://www.howtogeek.com/50432/how-to-install-php-on-iis-7-for-windows-server-2008/

How to install on a Linux Server

All Linux distributions come with PHP. However, it is recommended that you download the latest PHP source code, compile, and install on Linux. This will make it easier to upgrade PHP on an ongoing basis immediately after a new patch or release is available for download from PHP.

The Geek Stuff provides a great walk through of the process.

http://www.thegeekstuff.com/2008/07/instruction-guide-to-install-php5-from-source-on-linux/

Made in the USA
San Bernardino, CA
29 January 2015